RELATIONAL INTERCULTURAL COMMUNICATION FOR RELATIONAL INTERCULTURAL EDUCATION

Second Edition

Enoch Wan & Mark Hedinger

Relational Paradigm/Diaspora Series of CDRR

*Relational Intercultural Communication
for Relational Intercultural Education
Second Edition*

Copyright 2025 © Western Academic Publishers

Enoch Wan & Mark Hedinger

Cover designed by Mark Benec

ISBN: 978-1-954692-35-0

All rights reserved. Except for brief quotations in critical publications or reviews, no part of this book may be reproduced in any manner without prior written permission from the publisher or author.

Unless otherwise noted, Scripture quotations taken from the (NASB®) New American Standard Bible®, Copyright © 1960, 1971, 1977, by The Lockman Foundation. Used by permission. All rights reserved. lockman.org

CDRR (Center of Diaspora & Relational Research) @ https://www.westernseminary.edu/outreach/center-diaspora-relational-research

TABLE OF CONTENTS

LIST OF FIGURES vii
CHAPTER 1 INTRODUCTION 1
    The Background of this Book 3
    How to Use this Book 4
    Background of the Co-Authors 4
    The Purpose of this Book 5
    Definition of Key Terms 5
    The Readership and Organization of the Book 8
CHAPTER 2 AN OVERVIEW OF ICC 9
    Introduction 9
    Common Approaches to Communication and Intercultural Communication 9
    Review of Theories of Intercultural Communication 10
    The Challenges and Complexity of Intercultural Communication 15
    Communication from a Biblical/Scriptural perspective 19
    Conclusion 23
CHAPTER 3 THEORETICAL AND THEOLOGICAL FOUNDATION OF RELATIONAL INTERCULTURAL COMMUNICATION 25
    Introduction 25
    The Paradigm of Relational Interactionism 25
    Theological Foundation of RICC 27
    Communication within the Trinity 34
    Communication between the Trinity and humankind (vertical) 36
    Vertical Communication: Humanity's Communication to God 47
    Narrative Account of RICC & the Gospel (Jews + Gentile) 49
    Horizontal Communication 51
CHAPTER 4 The Relational Interactionist Communication (RICC) Approach 57
    Introducing the Paradigm of Relational Intercultural Communication (RICC) 58
    RICC: A Brief Introduction 58

A Closer Look at Four Phases of Communication in the RICC Model............ 67
Conclusion 93

CHAPTER 5 INTERCULTURAL RELATIONAL QUOTIENT (IRQ): TOWARDS GREATER INTERCULTURALITY IN INTERCULTURAL INTERACTIONS AND COMMUNICATION 95

Introduction 95
Intercultural Relational Quotient: Definition, Purpose, and Motivations ... 95
Current Approaches to Intercultural Interactions 97
A Terminological and Paradigmatic Shift 100
Theoretical Understandings of IRQ in RICC 104
IRQ and the Relational Intercultural Communication Paradigm 107
IRQ and Processes of Intercultural Communication 109
Developing IRQ for Greater RICC 111
IRQ in Intercultural Contexts 113
Conclusion 114

CHAPTER 6 Relational Communication for Relational Education: Part I COMMUNICATING ACROSS CULTURAL BARRIERS 115

Relational Communication in the Context of Relational Intercultural Education 115
Communication within Intercultural Education: 119
An Interactive Relational Approach 119
Conclusion 127

CHAPTER 7 Relational Communication for Relational Education: Part II TOWARD A MODEL OF RELATIONAL INTERCULTURAL EDUCATION FOR PROFESSIONAL DEVELOPMENT 129

Conclusion 137

CHAPTER 8 CASE STUDY: TOWARD THE DEVELOPMENT OF AN ANALYTICAL TOOL FOR RICC 139

Case Study of Education in India and the United States 139
Case study analysis 144
Conclusion 152

CONCLUSION	155
APPENDIX	159
BIBLIOGRAPHY	161

LIST OF FIGURES

Figure 1. Illustration of Cross-Cultural and Inter-cultural Communities 3
Figure 2. Two fundamental types of communication 10
Figure 3. Dynamic Revelation of the Trinity 28
Figure 4. Narrative Account of RICC and the Gospel to Jews & Gentile 51
Figure 5. Comparison/contrast between worldly and Trinitarian communication patterns 54
Figure 6. Interactive Relational Intercultural Communication 60
Figure 7. Interactive Model of Relational Communication 61
Figure 8. Perception and Human Senses 69
Figure 9. Perception and Culture 71
Figure 10. Social Interaction and Communication 76
Figure 11. Communication Patterns across Cultures 79
Figure 12. Communication and Volition 84
Figure 13. Factors that Influence Expression 88
Figure 14. Four Phases of Relational Interactive Communication 92
Figure 15. Comparison of Intercultural Competence and Intercultural Relational Quotient 103
Figure 16. Relational Communication in Intercultural Education 117
Figure 17. Being, Belonging, Becoming and Communication 122
Figure 18. A Relational Model of Individual Development 129
Figure 19. Relational Growth Process in Education 131
Figure 20. Personal attributes related to Relational Communication as seen in Amit A. Bhatia's case study 145
Figure 21. Group relational interactions seen in community through Amit A. Bhatia's case study 146
Figure 22. Communication cycle for educational development 147
Figure 23. "Being" in Jewish and Gentile Believers in Acts 15:1-35 149
Figure 24. "Belonging" in Jewish and Gentile Believers 150
Figure 25. Becoming in Jewish and Gentile Believers in Acts 15:1 - 35 152

CHAPTER 1
INTRODUCTION

Acts 17:28 – "in Him we live (belonging) and move (becoming) and have our being (being)."

This is a book about what lies between personal Beings/beings in terms of interaction and communication, i.e. between the Triune God and His people, and with other people groups. The topic of this book is "intercultural communication", but our relational approach is markedly different from other publications on the same topic, which generally deal with intercultural competencies and insights needed by people who give and receive messages across cultures. The popular approach to the study of "intercultural communication" tends to be mechanistic, individualistic and pragmatic. Yet there is another element to communication that is largely untapped: the process and pattern of relational interactions that occur between the communicating parties, leading to formation of personal relationships at individual and collective levels.

In this volume we will begin to develop a model of intercultural communication from that relational interactive perspective. We call the model **"Relational Intercultural Communication"**, (RICC).

In the simplest of cases, you could picture RICC as two people with a line between them. Traditional intercultural communication studies would focus on the two people themselves. The goal would be to increase or improve communication by improved knowledge, skill or attitude developed by one or all of the people involved.

What interests us, though, is not just those two parties. We are interested in the line between them – the connection that exists between the two parties. Even more, we see this relationship as both vertical and horizontal – as always including the involvement of Triune God (which we will call "vertical communication") as well as the interaction between people and other created beings, which we will call "horizontal communication."

You can think of examples in your own life, I am sure, of times when the relationship between you and God or between you and another person was really a core issue in your communication. If that relationship was strained, then no message, no matter how simple, seemed to be understood. On the other hand, when those lines of interactive relationship were mutually influential and appropriately accepted in healthy directions, you probably experienced a sort of freedom about the communication process.

Over the coming chapters, we will explore this idea of interactive relational cross-cultural communication from several points of view. We will see, for example, how growth and transformation occur within relational groups. In previous works[1] we have introduced the process of "being-belonging-becoming" as a short-hand for relational transformation.[2] We will see how RICC intersects with being-belonging-becoming.

We will also see the elements that are essential for RICC to take place. As one simple illustration, we recognize that communication is demonstrated by some kind of response. What if there is no response? Was there really communication? We want to consider issues like mutuality and reciprocity as parts of the RICC model.

Another element essential for RICC has to do with a comparison of cross-cultural with inter-cultural, and how those ideas interact with deliberate communication goals compared to a description of interactions which include various cultures.

Paula Schriefer[3] helps with this level of cross-cultural interaction by looking at it from a society-wide perspective. In her model, cross-cultural societies (or communities) have a standard, majority culture against which all other cultures are measured. Intercultural societies and communities, on the other hand, deliberately seek to develop respect and understanding for all of the cultures involved. Figure 1 illustrates the important distinctions that are seen in Schriefer's blog post.

As we move through our study of RICC, we will see places where there is deliberate interaction across cultures, seeking to build understanding with all of the possible cultures in a given context. On the other hand, we recognize the fact that in many multicultural situations, a majority culture is described as the standard of measure and "becoming" part of that majority culture is considered to be the unstated goal of all other community members. This descriptive view of cultural interaction, which Schriefer labels as "cross-cultural" is not our intention. We wish to promote a

---

[1] Please see Appendix 1 for a list of works by the authors of this text that are related to relational interactionism.

[2] See Enoch Wan and Jon Raibley, *Transformational Change in Christian Ministry*, 2nd edition. (Portland, OR: Western Academic Publishers, 2022). and Enoch Wan, Mark Hedinger, and Jon Raibley, *Transformational Growth: Intercultural Leadership/Discipleship/Mentorship* (Western Academic Publishers, 2023).

[3] Paula Schriefer, "What's the Difference between Multicultural, Intercultural, and Cross-Cultural Communication?," April 18, 2016, https://springinstitute.org/whats-difference-multicultural-intercultural-cross-cultural-communication/.

perspective on communication that is deliberately aiming at a growing, mutual level of understanding across the communities that are interacting.

The nomenclature in RICC will not necessarily always follow Schriefer's use of "intercultural" and "cross-cultural" but the aim of this book is intentional communication that builds deep understanding and respect within the cultures that are interacting.

Figure 1. Illustration of Cross-cultural and Inter-cultural Communities

Another perspective that we will take in developing the idea of RICC is to see communication in four phases: perception, conception, volition and expression. Those phases of communication will open the door for us to better understand the effects of things like previous experience, physical context, personal willingness to engage with others, and life goals on the development of relational intercultural communication.

Finally, this book will pay particular attention to the outworking of the RICC model in the area of education. There are many disciplines that involve communication across cultures. This book, though, will focus on RICC as it is expressed in relational interactive education.

Our exploration of RICC will end with case studies of communication across cultures, seeing in them some real-life examples of relational interactive communication.

The Background of this Book

Two strong influences make up the background of this book. The first is found in the growing body of work on relational interactionism. The second background to note is the contextual reality of the 21st Century.

This book has grown from the foundational concepts in Enoch Wan's original work on the "relational paradigm." That idea has, over the years and through the interaction of many students and mission practitioners, grown into what we now call "relational interactionism." At the same time, application of this relational school of thought has grown into the concept we call "interculturality," an idea that extends beyond normal ideas of intercultural competence. You can find extensive references in the bibliography and appendix to follow the development of these ideas.

In terms of the contextual background to this book, we refer to the simultaneous growth of two worldviews: methodological outworking of modernity on one side, and the postmodern refusal to recognize traditional categories on the other hand. The result of these two competing worldviews is a high level of confusion and intercultural stress. People genuinely are at a loss to understand the world they/we live in.

Biblical insight through a vertical relationship with Father, Son and Spirit becomes, in that confusion, a lighthouse to guide through the fog. The light that guides is a view into relationship that is at once both vertical and horizontal.

For both the theory and application/practice of RICC, we look to Scripture. The "tag line" for this book comes from Acts 17:28. When Paul was explaining a relational God to the Greek and Roman civilizations of his day, he explained in terms that are relational to their core. We know and understand this Triune God because "in Him we live and move and have our being." In the context of 21st century confusion and rootlessness, then, we present RICC with the hope that many around the globe will enter vertical and horizontal relationships that will lead them to a realization that indeed it is in Triune God that we "live and move and have our being."

How to Use this Book

RICC is written as a foundational textbook for Christian workers serving in cross-cultural situations as practitioners, teachers, and/or as theoreticians. Best use of the text will take place in contexts that promote

1. dialog and discussion between people from differing cultural backgrounds.
2. Interaction specifically focused on application to real-life intercultural situations, so that communication can be considered as part of the intercultural response to those real-life situations.

Background of the Co-Authors

Enoch Wan has served on the faculty at Western Seminary for twenty-one years, leading three doctoral programs in intercultural studies and intercultural education. He served for two terms as president of the Evangelical Missiological Society and as vice president in various capacities for two decades. Enoch began his research on two paradigms (i.e., relational realism and diaspora missiology) during his sabbatical as scholar-in-residence at Yale Divinity School over two decades ago. Since then, he has published many articles and dozens of books on these two themes.

Mark Hedinger came to this book project after a long history of mission work and study. After living and working in Mexico for twelve years, Mark served in mid-level leadership of a mission agency. In those roles he became convinced of the importance of intercultural training for mission practitioners. After completing a doctorate at Western Seminary under the direction of Dr. Enoch Wan, he eventually joined a mission training program headquartered in Portland, Oregon. That organization, now named CultureBound, offers training for intercultural ministry and second language acquisition to intercultural workers sent out from many different nations. Mark also continues to teach intercultural communication and education through Western Seminary and other schools.

The key idea that ties Mark together with Dr. Wan and the intercultural programs at Western is a commitment to the relational perspective. They are convinced that life and ministry are much more aligned with relationships than with methods and techniques. That idea is central to all elements of the collaboration between Drs. Wan and Hedinger.

For the sake of readability, "I" is used instead of "we."

The Purpose of this Book

The purpose of this book is three-fold:

1. To propose a relational-interactionist approach to intercultural communication which we call RICC.
2. To distinguish how RICC is similar and yet distinct from more common approaches to intercultural communication.
3. To apply that relational-interactionist approach to intercultural communication in the specific area of intercultural education.

Definition of Key Terms

Culture

The context/consequence of patterned interaction of personal Beings/beings, in contrast to the popular usage of the term referring solely to the presumed closed system of *Homo sapiens*. This definition of culture can be applied or referred to angelic (fallen or good) beings of the angel-culture and the dynamic interaction of the Three Persons of the Triune God in theo-culture.[4]

---

[4] Wan and Raibley, *Transformational Change in Christian Ministry*, 5–6.

Education
The process of interaction between the teacher/trainer/instructor and the student/trainee/learner during which the latter is transformed relationally in multiple dimensions; cognitive, affective and behavioral.

Intercultural Communication (ICC) and **Relational Intercultural Communication** (RICC)
- The foundation to ICC and RICC is the term "communication" which is defined as "the process between two or more beings/Beings of creating and interpreting messages that seek to elicit a response, and which include both horizontal and vertical interactions.[5]"
- "Intercultural Communication (ICC) is the process between two or more beings/Beings of creating and interpreting messages that seek to elicit a response, and which include both horizontal and vertical interactions that cross from one set of cultural patterns to another."
- "Relational Intercultural Communication (RICC) is the <u>relational</u> process between two or more beings/Beings of creating and interpreting messages that seek to elicit a response, and which include both horizontal and vertical interactions that occur between the varied patterns of life displayed by members of different cultural groups."

Relational intercultural education
- RICE is defined as a "Christian educator participating in God's *missio Dei*[6] to nurture unity (with cultural diversity), mutuality (in communion and sharing), harmony (*shalom*[7] - in spite of ethnic diversity), reciprocity (overcoming barriers, e.g. intercultural communication) amidst interaction of personal Beings/beings within an intercultural context.

---

[5] Adapted from Em Griffin, Andrew M. Ledbetter, and Glenn G. Sparks, *A First Look at Communication Theory 10th Edition*, 10th edition. (McGraw-Hill Education, 2018).

[6] The definition of "mission" is "a process by which Christians (individuals) and the Church (institutional) continue on and carry out the *missio Dei* of the Triune God ("mission") at both individual and institutional levels spiritually (saving souls) and socially (ushering in *shalom*) for redemption, reconciliation, and transformation (Enoch Yee-nock Wan, *Diaspora Missiology: Theory, Methodology, and Practice*, 2nd ed. Portland, Or.: Institute of Diaspora Studies : Western Seminary, 2014). For Enoch Wan's detailed discussion on the definition of "mission," see Enoch Wan, "'Mission' and '*Missio Dei*': Response to Charles van Engen's 'Mission Defined and Described,'" in *MissionShift: Global Mission Issues in the Third Millennium*, eds. David J. Hesselgrave and Ed Stetzer, (Nashville: B & H Publishing Group, 2010), 41-50.

[7] *"shalom"* is the context of total wellness in which created humanity can reach his/her full potential and properly respond to God and His message relationally (Jer. 29:7, 1 Tim. 2:1-5).

- In the context of education, RICE is "the formal/informal/non-formal process whereby the educator interacts relationally with the learner towards development/enrichment in 'being' and 'doing' (i.e. multidimensional such as cognitive, affective, volitional... etc.) within a cross-cultural context."[8]

Intercultural educator
An educator who operates between two or more cultures with an intercultural self-perception and orientation.

Interculturality
Instead of being monocultural, interculturality is both the commitment and competence of someone venturing beyond his/her cultural background and boundary with multidimensional qualities, such as self-identity (psychological), multiculturality (ideational), intentionality (attitudinal) and practicality (operational). Thus, "interculturality" is the quality of an ideal intercultural teacher/trainer, including:

- A subjective construction of identity (psychological)
- A desire to embrace "multiculturality" as a goal for growth (growth-orientation)
- The ability to navigate among different cultural spaces (cultural aptitude)
- Competence in two or more languages (linguistic aptitude)
- The ability to relate and interact harmoniously with those who are culturally diverse[9] ("shalomic reality")[10]

Intercultural Ministry (ICM)
Christian ministry carried out within a cross-cultural context.

Relational Interactionism (RI)
An interdisciplinary narrative framework that develops from practical considerations of dynamic interaction of personal Beings/beings, forming realistic relational networks in multiple contexts (i.e., theo-culture, angel-culture and human-culture) and with various consequences.[11]

---

[8] Enoch Wan, "Interculturality and Intercultural Education: The Concept and Definition of 'Culture' at Two Levels" (Western Seminary, 2022), 10.

[9] David Luna, Torsten Ringberg, and Laura A. Peracchio, "One Individual, Two Identities: Frame Switching among Biculturals," *Journal of Consumer Research* 35, no. 2 (August 1, 2008): 279–293, accessed October 3, 2024, https://doi.org/10.1086/586914.

[10] See Enoch Wan and Jace Cloud, *Doxological Missiology: Theory, Motivation, and Practice* (Western Academic Publishers, 2022).

[11] Enoch Wan, "Rethinking Urban Mission in Terms of Spiritual and Social Transformational Change" (Virtual: Missiological Society of Ghana/WAMS Biennial International Conference, October 26, 2021).

Intercultural Relational Quotient (IRQ)
IRQ is defined as a measure of an individual's ability to nurture and maintain depth and influence in interactions with others in a cultural context outside of the one(s) to which the individual belongs.

Transformational Growth (TG)
The dynamism and process of positive change, originated vertically from the Triune God and ushered in the relational reality horizontally, through the process of interaction between personal Beings (the Triune God) and human beings (at micro and macro levels) multi-dimensionally (i.e. with spiritual, moral, social, and behavioral dimensions at personal and/or institutional levels).[12]

Transgressional Change (TC)
Change caused by the dynamism of the enemy of the Triune God and by the fallen nature that is contrary to the attributes of God and His will, His Lordship as revealed through the Incarnate and Inspired Word, Jesus Christ and the Scripture, i.e., the opposite of transformational change.[13]

The Readership and Organization of the Book

This is an introductory textbook for teachers and trainers serving interculturally, with a focus on integrating the understanding of "relational intercultural communication" (RICC) for the practice of "relational intercultural education." (RICE)

The book is organized around "growth" through relationship-building in communication:

- First, we consider the idea of communication and intercultural communication as seen in most intercultural studies textbooks and course offerings.
- Second, we will develop the idea of relational communication and follow that with the idea of relational intercultural communication (RICC).
- Third, in the theoretical portion of the book we will expand RICC into the specific context of intercultural education.

Finally, case studies will be presented that highlight and illustrate the concept and usefulness of RICC in educational settings.

---

[12] Wan, Hedinger, and Raibley, *Transformational Growth*, 6.
[13] Wan, Hedinger, and Raibley, *Transformational Growth*, 6.

CHAPTER 2
AN OVERVIEW OF ICC

Introduction

In this chapter, we will provide an overview of intercultural communication in anticipation of the coverage on RICC in chapter 3.

Common Approaches to Communication and Intercultural Communication

Em Griffin's 10th edition introductory textbook of communication science starts with the observation that trying to define what is meant by communication is notoriously difficult.[14] The authors quote a researcher from 50 years ago who cataloged over 120 different definitions of communication, noting that in the following 50 years, many new definitions have also been suggested.

When we look at the range of topics that are covered in communication textbooks and courses, we see why Griffin and his colleagues would make their statement. The study of communication ranges from methods of communication, media used to send and/or receive a message, factors involved when the communication takes place within specialized fields of study or within specific groups of people, the level of technical language used in the communication, and on and on. Ironically, we seem to have trouble communicating about what we mean by "communication". The paragraphs below will provide more detail about the range of meaning that is used in the study of "communication". We will then suggest a definition of communication for the purposes of this textbook.

Two Types of Communication

At the root of these different ways of considering communication, from a biblical perspective we suggest that there are only two types of communication: objectifying and authentic. Figure 2 shows the contrast in terms of presentation and orientation, process and possible outcome. Later in this chapter we will consider other ways of classifying the different types of communication. The two types in Figure 2, though, point to a fundamental distinction. Communication is either set to serve self or serve God and His purposes. As Jesus said, our words are meant to either be "yes or no" (Matthew 5:37). All else is from the evil one. The "objectifying communication" serves self, communicating with people to fulfill what is in one's self-interest. We use the term "objectifying" because essentially such

---

[14] Griffin, Ledbetter, and Sparks, *A First Look at Communication Theory 10th Edition*, 5–9.

communication flows from a point of view that sees other people and even God as objects which fulfill one's own wishes.[15]

In contrast, authentic human interaction says "yes" or "no" depending on the situation. It seeks to honestly, transparently create genuine interaction.

We will see various schools of thought about communication. They can all be used toward godly or ungodly ends. The kind of communication is not in question; the more fundamental issue is the desired goal: self-interest, or service to others.

TYPES / FEATURE	OBJECTIFYING COMMUNICATION	AUTHENTIC HUMAN INTERACTION
Presentation & Orientation	• polished narrative • calculated communication	• transparency • authenticity
Process	• exploitation of social media • image projection	• open dialogue • relational interaction
Possible outcome	• pretentious communication • manipulated outcome • self-serving & exploitative	• genuine relational interaction • mutually edifying (horizontal) • God-honoring (vertical)
Goal	• Maximize "success" for one's self-interest	• To know and be known vertically and horizontally

Figure 2. Two fundamental types of communication

Review of Theories of Intercultural Communication

A review of communication textbooks and teaching syllabi shows what seems to be a wide range of theories of communication. And yet, there are only a few models for describing intercultural communication, each with numerous variations. Some authors focus on the mechanics of how a message is shared between people. Others focus on social factors like

---

[15] Arthur C. Brooks, *From Strength to Strength: Finding Success, Happiness, and Deep Purpose in the Second Half of Life* (New York: Portfolio, 2022), 45.

relative economic or political power. Still other communication texts look at the relationship patterns between members of a group.

In considering the different ways that scholars and writers talk about communication, we suggest that a basic series of questions will help to make sense of this array of communication theories. Basic questions which organize communication theories are presented below, along with a small number of examples.

Communication Theories Organized by Guiding Questions

1. **How many** people are involved in the communication? (considering the issues of interpersonal communication, group communication, and mass communication).
2. **Who** is involved in the communication? (relevant to political communication, persuasive communication, intercultural communication, intergenerational communication)
3. **What** is the topic being communicated? (relevant to educational communication, medical communication, legal communication).
4. **What language** is used for the communication? (relevant to intercultural communication, translation theories in communication, linguistics as it affects communication).
5. **When** is the communication occurring? (relevant to time-structured communication like news programs or church services).
6. **Where** is the communication taking place? (relevant to intercultural communication and to contextual factors in communication).
7. **Why** is the communication taking place? (Relevant to persuasive communication vs. informative vs. emotive vs imaginary. Consider the differences between a poem, a math lecture, and an advertisement that seeks to persuade consumers to buy a product).
8. **What is the relationship** between the members of the communication? Do the speaker and listener know each other? Are there multiple parties involved as listeners? As speakers? Are there different levels of social influence between the people involved? (relevant to the field of relational communication and issues of power-dynamics in communication).
9. **Which medium** is being used for the communication? (relevant to media decisions for example: painting, photography, cooking, clothing design, poetry, music all point to different media, and each can be used for communication).

Distinct Schools of Thought

Within this array of basic questions, there are a few distinct schools of thought that deserve special attention.

1. Most communication approaches look at the use of signs and symbols as the key issue in communication. This semiotics school of thought understands that people use words or other symbols to recreate in the mind of one person what is already in the mind of the speaker. When the semiotics approach is extended to a large audience, it uses "mass communication" as a tool to extend that message. Whether the audience is small or large, the semiotics school of thought will focus on the message itself and the signs, words, symbols that recreate the message from the speaker to the hearer.[16]

2. The interactive relational communication approach that is presented by Rogers and Escudero[17] is unique in that it does not focus on the message, nor on the individuals who are participating in the communicative dyad. The focus of Rogers and Escudero is the relationship that is formed between the people and subsequently, on the communication patterns that develop between them. As they say in their text, "Social relationships lie at the heart of our humanness, and in turn, communication lies at the heart of our relationships. In constructing the social worlds we inhabit, there is an intimate tie between communication and relationship, with each interwoven in the other. This interconnection represents an underlying premise of the relational communication perspective. Thus, while it is assumed that our relationships contextualize and influence our lives, it is also assumed that our relationships are constituted and shaped through our communication processes."[18]

This relational interactive approach is important for our purposes because it focuses on individual people in relationship to one another rather than focusing on the more generalized culture from which those individuals come. Authors Edwin Hoffman and Arjan Verdooren state, "The focus of this book is on intercultural *interaction*; encounters between people of different cultural backgrounds. This means that we do not take culture *as such* as the

---

[16] Paul G Hiebert, *Cultural Anthropology* (Philadelphia: Lippincott, 1976), 113–137.
[17] L. Edna Rogers and Valentin Escudero, eds., *Relational Communication: An Interactional Perspective To the Study of Process and Form*, 1st edition. (Mahwah, NJ: Routledge, 2003), Chapter 1: Theoretical Foundations.
[18] Rogers and Escudero, *Relational Communication*, Chapter 1.

starting point, but rather the interactions between individuals with different cultural backgrounds.[19]" (emphasis in the original).

3. There is another large distinction between the study of communication in general compared to the study of communication that is specifically intercultural. This distinction calls for understanding of how communication patterns and meanings vary across cultures, and what it means to communicate when there are differences in social and cultural expectations.[20]

As in the semiotics approach, it is the message that is foremost in this intercultural communication realm. However, there is a difference in that the meaning attributed to that message in one cultural group may be quite different than the meaning attributed within another cultural group. One wants for "the message" to be clearly communicated, even though the audience follows patterns of thought, speech and communication that are distinct from the presenter's cultural norms. The concept of contextualization is aimed at helping communicators from one culture to use the audience's communication patterns and symbols to approximate meanings between sender and receiver.[21]

4. Another distinct school of thought is focused on the different messages that are expressed and perceived based on the differences within the audience. Justice or economic issues, for instance, become the focus of communication studies. Educational levels also can help distinguish one audience from another. Language interpreters and/or translators refer to the appropriate register of language so that it may be understood by a particular audience. This is message-centric communication prepared for a specific audience or context depending on their language ability[22].

---

[19] Dr Edwin Hoffman and Arjan Verdooren, *Diversity Competence: Cultures Don't Meet, People Do*, Illustrated edition. (Wallingford ; Boston: CABI, 2019), 19.

[20] Everett M Rogers and Thomas M Steinfatt, *Intercultural Communication* (Long Grove, IL: Waveland Press, Inc., 1999).

[21] Timothy Tennent, *Theology in the Context of World Christianity*. Grand Rapids, MI: Zondervan, 2007. Pages 198-199 are particularly helpful in describing the dangers found where contextualization is poorly done: syncretism on one hand, and ethnocentric extractionism on the other. Also, A. Scott Moreau, *Contextualization in World Mission* (Grand Rapids: Kregel Academic, 2012) gives a helpful guide to six conceptual guides for contextualization: indigeneity, transformation, syncretism, incarnation, holism, and praxis.

[22] David Katan and Mustapha Taibi, *Translating Cultures: An Introduction for Translators, Interpreters and Mediators*, 3rd edition. (Routledge, 2021).

There are levels of truth and usefulness in the different models of communication that we have mentioned. Yet there are also weaknesses in these models. For example:

We certainly communicate from one person to another, and we are important actors in those communications. Yet we are not the only communicators. God is also there, opening or closing minds and hearts (for example, Acts 16:14 and Luke 24:27-32).

Likewise, we use words and signs and symbols to communicate. It is important that we order our thoughts well and that we choose our words carefully with respect to our audience. We all know the power of art and the power of poetry. We recognize the important communication that takes place through a good meal or through music. Those signs and symbols are powerful, but at the same time, they are not universally understood. At least three important factors affect our communication with words, signs and symbols:

1. There is a God who enters the human heart and opens our understanding, even beyond the words used. As Jesus was walking with the disciples along the road to Emmaus (Luke 24), He explained to them the flow of Old Testament history. Another example comes from Acts 16. When Lydia heard the Word of God preached by Paul, "The Lord opened her heart." Communication includes the involvement of Triune God who opens our understanding of His Word even beyond the words used by human teachers. Paul's prayer in Ephesians 1:17-18 is staggering in this implication – Paul prays that God would give wisdom and revelation in the knowledge of God, that the saints might know the hope and riches we have in God.

   We could likewise think of Pharoah, whose heart was closed by his own decision first, and later by God (Exodus 7:3 – 4 cf Ex 10:20).

   The fact is that God communicates through many means, including His work to open and close human understanding.

2. Another matter that affects human communication is the question of intercultural communication. Different cultural groups have their own patterns of communication. Besides the obvious question of which languages are used, we also see different values, organizational expectation, understanding of metaphors, patterns of thought, and on and on. Those different cultural patterns affect communication to the point that a person may understand the individual words used in an intercultural exchange, but entirely misinterpret the meaning. With intercultural communication comes not only the challenge inherent in

communication itself, but those "normal" communications are complicated by patterns that differ from one culture to the other.
3. Finally, there is the issue of volition. People enter communication based on their will to do so. To see communication of any sort as a technique or method will miss the fact that humanly, we all hear what we want to hear.

The Challenges and Complexity of Intercultural Communication

Moving past the description and definition of intercultural communication, we want to consider some examples of the practical real-world situations where intercultural communication is important. These situations, illustrated below, are found in everyday life around the world. The point is that we need both a strong theory of intercultural relational communication and a strong practical ability to live it out, too.

The Nature of Communication within and across Cultural Divides

Intercultural communication does not exist only as theory; it is a reality in the everyday life of millions of people. For example:

Multicultural churches which look to develop worship, fellowship, mutual care, outreach and growing biblical knowledge with people from different cultural backgrounds. Some of those outcomes are easily accomplished across cultures but there are others that have proven difficult to span.

Cross-cultural missions often create situations that call for cross cultural communication. It might be an expat who is speaking into the cultural practices of the host group. It can also be missionaries from multiple backgrounds who are serving together in yet another ministry culture.

Multicultural mission teams bring their own intercultural communication challenges. From experience, we[23] have witnessed intercultural/cross-cultural stress within ministry teams over questions like,

- Which holidays should be celebrated?
- What foods are best for team meetings?
- What are the expectations for leadership or decision-making within the diverse group?

Intercultural communication also shows up due to the migration of culture (quite beyond the migration of people): sushi, tacos and hamburgers are all available at your local food court. Indian and Mexican poetry is available at your local bookstore. Al Jazeera, the NY Times and the Economist are provided on your news feed. Intercultural communication is not only

---

[23] For ease of reading, many personal illustrations in this volume will be expressed with pronouns "I" or "we."

interested in the movement of people from one place to another; it is also interested in the diffusion of language, foods, music, and other communication media.

These illustrations of intercultural communication point toward the nature of our relationship with culture. When we are within our own culture, we have an implicit understanding of the patterns of the people. When we move into an unfamiliar culture that implicit knowledge disappears. We did not grow up in that cultural milieu therefore we have to deliberately learn what is intuitive to our neighbors. Think of all the manners and customs and habits of thought and language that a kindergartner knows simply because they grew up in their homeland. The adult moving into a new culture does not share in those levels of understanding. That adult needs to deliberately learn the customs, values, expressions and beliefs that insiders learned as young children.

There are other factors that affect intercultural communication besides the nature of communication. We will look at six issues which complicate our intercultural communication: human will, faulty thinking, lack of skill, lack of knowledge, personal inflexibility, and above all a lack of faith that God is also involved.

The Heart Attitude Problem

One of the biggest issues in intercultural communication is the question of human will; that is, volition. Simply put, do the people involved *want* to understand one another?

There are reasons why a person might not wish to communicate with people from another culture. There are also reasons why a person might be willing to communicate if it happens easily, but unwilling to invest significant resources of time, energy or emotional involvement. Some of the heart issues that negatively affect intercultural communication include:

- Prejudice against the other people group.
- Pressure from one's own group to not engage with the other group.
- A point of view that assumes one's own culture is superior to others. This assumed superiority of one's own culture is referred to as "ethnocentric."[24]
- A feeling that if any efforts are necessary, it is the responsibility of the other group to make the effort.

---

[24] Milton Bennett, "Developmental Model of Intercultural Sensitivity (DMIS)," *International Journal of Intercultural Relations* 10, no. 2 (n.d.): 179–196.

The Thinking Problem

There are two ways that wrong thinking that can make it difficult to communicate across cultures.

The Fallacy of False Consensus is the wrong assumption that "other people see life as I do; we have similar beliefs and values, and our behaviors will be similar in any given context."[25] This fallacy leads people to minimize the importance of cross-cultural or intercultural communication because, the thinking goes, those other people will naturally think and act as I do anyway.

The Fallacy of Composition is equally damaging in intercultural settings. This is the wrong thinking that assumes that what is true of one member of a group is equally true of all other members. This is the thinking that erroneously builds stereotypes; if one person from that other culture has a particular characteristic, then (the thinking goes), all will. Of course, stated in this way we can see the errors of the fallacy. But in real-life situations people will quickly create stereotypes which categorize entire groups of people because of the actions of a few.

The Skill Problem

We have approached the idea of intercultural communication from the perspective that it is more than a competence, and that is true. But it is not less than competence; in other words, there are areas of skill, knowledge and attitude that undergird successful intercultural relationships.

Some of the skills that are necessary for intercultural engagement include:

- The ability to observe by using multiple media types.
- The ability to ask good questions.
- The ability to see patterns of thought, behavior and attitude in the lives of people from another culture.
- The ability to creatively see how basic human needs are met through the patterns of an unfamiliar culture.
- The ability to relate to people from home culture as well as other cultures, and to learn more about the common patterns of the people through those interpersonal relationships.

---

[25] Lee Ross, David Greene, and Pamela House, "The 'False Consensus Effect': An Egocentric Bias in Social Perception and Attribution Processes," *Journal of Experimental Social Psychology* 13, no. 3 (May 1977): 279–301, accessed October 4, 2024, https://linkinghub.elsevier.com/retrieve/pii/002210317790049X.

The Knowledge Problem

Effective intercultural communication includes a substantial knowledge factor. Unfortunately, this knowledge factor is too often seen as the only real requirement for intercultural communication. It is as if we think that the ability to memorize the Individualism/Collectivism definitions, and keep in mind which countries show "high power distance" is all that is needed to succeed in an intercultural environment. We want to quickly say that there is more to intercultural communication than only knowledge. But we also agree that knowledge is important and should be learned. Some of the important pieces of knowledge that need to be grasped include:

- How high context communication differs from low context communication.
- How literate, text-based communication styles differ from oral styles.
- The different ways that emotion is expressed across cultures
- How people think differently, including the connection between language and perception, ordering of thoughts from universal to particular, and the categories that people use for organizing their lives.
- The different ways that nonverbal communication can be seen.
- The cultural dimensions of Hofstede[26], Trompenaars[27], Meyer[28], etc.
- Some of the ways that education varies across cultures

The Human Problem

Intercultural communication, no matter how complex, comes back to people from differing cultural backgrounds who are interacting. In other words, there are all kinds of personalities involved. Within that panorama of personality, one particularly important issue is the idea of flexibility.

The Intercultural Readiness Check[29] has applied quantitative research methods to identify the personal characteristics that are most important for predicting successful intercultural involvement. They found four elements, each with two subdivisions. Taken as a whole, looking at the range of

---

[26] Geert Hofstede, Gert Jan Hofstede, and Michael Minkov, *Cultures and Organizations: Software of the Mind, Third Edition*, 3 edition. (New York: McGraw-Hill Education, 2010).

[27] Alfons Trompenaars and Charles Hampden-Turner, *Riding the Waves of Culture: Understanding Diversity in Global Business* (London; Boston: Nicholas Brealey Publishing, 2015).

[28] Erin Meyer, *The Culture Map* (New York: PublicAffairs, 2016).

[29] Intercultural Readiness Check website https://interculturalreadiness.com/. Accessed January 7, 2025.

expression within these areas helps us to gauge the personal flexibility that a person might naturally display. [30]

Intercultural Sensitivity
    Includes cultural awareness and attention to signals

Intercultural Communication
    Includes active listening and adapting to differing communication styles

Building Commitment
    Includes building relationships and reconciling stakeholder needs

Managing Uncertainty
    Includes openness to cultural diversity and exploring new approaches.

The Faith Problem

Generally speaking, people see communication in human terms; the interactions that we have called "horizontal." But the model we propose includes vertical relationships and vertical communication. We assume that God is active and that He is involved in communication in a multitude of ways. One of the challenges of intercultural communication is the faith problem of knowing that God wants us to be actively involved in communication, and yet also having faith that He will bring about the results that He intends. For example, consider Acts 16:14 where the Lord opened Lydia's heart to accept the things that Paul had spoken. Other Scriptural passages speak of other ways that God is involved in communicating, especially the communication of His Word. Faith in the promise that God will work in and through the communication of His Word is essential for proper understanding of communication.

    "So shall My word be which goes forth from My mouth; It shall not return to Me empty without accomplishing what I desire and without succeeding in the matter for which I sent it." (Isaiah 55:11).

    This promise and trusting in the active involvement of God is just as significant in intercultural communication as it is in intra-cultural communication.

Communication from a Biblical/Scriptural perspective

So far, we have looked at several of the sources from which RICC grows. We have seen common approaches to communication and specifically intercultural communication. We have also considered the challenges and complexities that are part of any discussion of intercultural communication.

---

[30] Ursula Brinkmann and Oscar van Weerdenburg, *Intercultural Readiness: Four Competences for Working across Cultures*, 2014, 36.

We have seen Scriptural truth involved at points throughout our discussion. Now, we want to dig deeper into theological perspectives that affect RICC.

Francis Schaeffer builds his case for a Christian worldview based on a God who exists and who communicates.[31] Schaeffer makes the point that God's communication is far deeper than simply the expression of facts. God communicates in the Bible through propositional facts, but He also goes beyond that and communicates about His very Being. "The Bible teaches in two different ways: first it teaches certain things in didactic statements, in verbalizations, in propositions... Second, the Bible teaches by showing how God works in the world that He Himself made."[32] That communication of God as Creator and as actively involved within His creation is tied to another important point of revelation. God communicates about His own character.[33] As Schaeffer puts it, "He told us what His character is, and this becomes our moral law, our moral standard."[34]

Schaeffer's understanding of communication includes more than just his analysis of God's communication in both didactic and character-describing ways. Schaeffer also looks at how this God who communicates is the God who created mankind to communicate.

> Christianity's presupposition begins with a God who is there, who is the infinite-personal God, who has made man in His image. He has made man to be a verbalizer in the area of propositions in his horizontal communication to other men. Even secular anthropologists say that somehow or other, they do not know why, man is a verbalizer. You have something different in man. The Bible says, and the Christian position says, I can tell you why: God is a personal-infinite God. There has always been communication, before the creation of all else, in the Trinity. And God has made man in His own image, and part of making man in His own image is that man is a verbalizer. That stands in the unity of the Christian structure.[35]

There is one last link in Schaeffer's argument. Not only does God communicate in multiple ways, and not only did God create mankind to also

---

[31] Francis Schaeffer, *The Complete Works of Francis A Schaeffer: Volume 1: A Christian View of Philosophy and Culture.* (Westchester IL: Crossway Books, 1982).

[32] Schaeffer, *The Complete Works of Francis A Schaeffer: Volume 1: A Christian View of Philosophy and Culture.*, 336.

[33] Schaeffer, *The Complete Works of Francis A Schaeffer: Volume 1: A Christian View of Philosophy and Culture.*, 303.

[34] Schaeffer, *The Complete Works of Francis A Schaeffer: Volume 1: A Christian View of Philosophy and Culture.*, 303.

[35] Schaeffer, *The Complete Works of Francis A Schaeffer: Volume 1: A Christian View of Philosophy and Culture.*, 326.

communicate, but this God of communication and of creation is also the God who created relationships.

> The infinite-personal God who exists – not just an abstraction- made things in correlation that the early scientists had courage to expect to find out the explanation of the universe. The God who is there made the universe, with things together, in relationships. Indeed, the whole area of science turns upon the fact that He has made a world in which things are made to stand together, that there are relationships between things. So God made the external universe which makes true science possible, but He also made man and made him to live in that universe. He did not make man to live somewhere else. So we have three things coming together: God, the infinite-personal God, who made the universe, and man whom he made to live in that universe, and the Bible which He has given us to tell us about that universe. Are we surprised that there is a unity between them? Why should we be surprised?[36]

Any study of communication, including intercultural communication, is only complete when it includes both horizontal and vertical communication, and when it goes beyond simple proposition and includes the self-revealing nature of God's communication to humankind. A full view into communication will also consider the relationship between God the Creator and mankind the created, including the amazing truth that humanity was created in God's image, which leads to our ability to communicate as we do.

Continuing to look at what the Bible says about communication, we also want to extend our view of horizontal communication. So far, we have approximated the idea of horizontal communication by considering it within the created beings that we call human beings. But there are other communicating beings which are also created.

Some of those created beings are loyal to God and are referred to as angels. Hebrews 1:5 and 1:14 explain that angels are thus ministering spirits. They communicate (for example Luke 1:19) and they serve God and His people.

Other created beings, though, have rebelled against God. They also communicate, but it is with the intention of exalting themselves and leading God's people astray. Isaiah 14:12-14 details the communication of one such rebellious creature, telling us how this "star of the morning, son of the dawn" said (note the communication involved) in his heart,

> I will ascend into heaven
> I will raise my throne above the stars of God

---

[36] Schaeffer, *The Complete Works of Francis A Schaeffer: Volume 1: A Christian View of Philosophy and Culture.*, 329.

I will sit on the mount of assembly
I will ascend above the heights of the clouds
I will make myself like the Most High

When this self-exaltation was communicated, it brought other created beings into similar rebellion, leading to "transgressional change."[37] Ephesians 6:12 identifies the enemies of Christ and His Church as "Rulers, powers, world forces of this darkness, against the spirituals forces of wickedness in the heavenly places". Clearly the idea of horizontal communication extends beyond just people. There are other created beings; some which honor and serve the Triune God, and others which rebel and transgress against God.

Looking at communication through both horizontal and vertical perspectives leads to the important conclusion that God is not limited to any particular "school of thought" regarding communication. Humanity communicates through the signs and symbols that we make into arts, language, music, food etc. We can be very subtle, for example using a tone of voice to change the meaning of words. But those subtle shifts are only variations in the same signs and symbols that our semiotics school of thought focuses on.

God, on the other hand, can and does communicate beyond signs and symbols. He used visions which went beyond words or symbols to communicate His message to the prophets of both Old and New Testament. He describes His ability to engage beyond words in Philippians 4:7 where He promises "peace that passes understanding" to those who present their prayers to Him. Our words spoken in prayer bring His response that goes beyond words. No human sign or symbol can capture that experience, and yet how many Christians can attest to His faithfulness in keeping that promise!

Humanity is limited in our communication. We rely on our physical senses to express and to receive. For the most part our communication with one another and even with God is presented through words, the arts, meals, music etc. that we fashion to be the signs and symbols recognized as the semiotic school of thought. God, though, is not limited and can communicate directly with our spirit (1 Corinthians chapter 2) or with the other members of the Trinity on our behalf (Romans 8:26). [38]

---

[37] Wan and Raibley, *Transformational Change in Christian Ministry*.
[38] This realization has significant hermeneutical implications. For instance, see *Beyond the Obvious*. James DeYoung and Sarah Hurty. Gresham, OR: Vision House Publishing Inc, 1995.

Conclusion

Intercultural Communication, as we have seen in this chapter, is a complex topic. The topic has been understood from the perspective of numerous schools of thought, and communication has a role in understanding many of mankind's problems. In addition to those sociological and anthropological perspectives, the Bible also speaks frequently to human communication, both vertically (communication between God and mankind) and horizontally (communication between people or other created beings). The distinction that underlies all of these perspectives is between communication aimed at objectifying God and people to simply serve one's own wishes, versus authentic communication that seeks to understand and be understood.

Conclusion

CHAPTER 3
THEORETICAL AND THEOLOGICAL FOUNDATION OF RELATIONAL INTERCULTURAL COMMUNICATION

Introduction

The next three chapters introduce the theoretical and theological foundation of "relational intercultural communication" (RICC). We will consider intercultural communication from a relational point of view, including these four perspectives.

1. The perspective of relational transformational growth as seen in the "Being-Belonging-Becoming" model.
2. The perspective of intercultural communication with its hallmarks of mutuality, reciprocity and schizogenesis.
3. The perspective of communication through the lens of perception-conception-volition-expression. This will be the longest portion of our model.
4. The interaction between relational intercultural communication and relational intercultural education.

The Paradigm of Relational Interactionism[39]

"Relational interactionism" (RI) is a paradigm within the social sciences. We have adapted this paradigm so that it emphasizes the importance of interaction of personal Beings (Divine, Creator)/beings (created) in both vertical and horizontal connections. These connections, or relationships, expand into networks by which we better understand socio-cultural phenomena. Relational Interactionism shifts the focus from static social structures to the dynamic interactions and connections that constitute social life. This approach offers a comprehensive framework for analyzing how:

    a. individual identities and social boundaries/entities are formed.
    b. pattern and process of relational interaction are to be examined.
    c. socio-cultural reality is best understood as dynamic, with changes occurring due to relational interaction of personal beings/Beings.
    d. socio-cultural reality is fluid and can be transformed (becoming) through a process of relational interaction in community (belonging) of personal beings/Beings.

---

[39] Readers who are interested in a general introduction to "relational interaction theory," please see Appendix 1.

Core Principles of Relational Interactionism (RI)

- **Relational Paradigm**: Relational interactionism posits that society is fundamentally composed of relationships rather than isolated individuals or static/fixed structures. This perspective challenges traditional sociological approaches by emphasizing the fluid and dynamic interconnected nature of social life.
- **Relationship, Networks and Social Integration**: The relational interactionist approach views social relationship as foundational and emergent networks as the primary units of analysis. It explores how these relational networks facilitate social integration and the emergence of social order. This perspective is particularly useful in narrating complex social phenomena and trends on a global scale.
- **Relational Realism and Relational Interactionism**: Relational realism provides the epistemological and ontological framework for relational interactionism. While critical realism focuses on the transformative potential of social structures,[40] RI provides a more nuanced understanding of social integration by viewing the social order in relational and interactive terms.

Applications and Implications of Relational Interactionism

- **Urban and Spatial Relationality**: Relational interactionism has been applied to study urban spaces and social interactions within them, highlighting the limitations of traditional views of ethnicity, the classic approach of urban studies, and methodological nationalism. These studies lead to the recognition of fluidity of social reality and emphasize the importance of studying the pattern and process of relational interactions.
- **Cultural and Network Research**: The paradigm has influenced network research by introducing a socio-cultural dimension, which examines how networks are not just static/structural but fluid and dynamic due to relational interactions.
- **Intercultural Studies**: Relational interaction can take place within an intercultural context; therefore, relational interactionism is helpful in studying the complexity of intercultural relationships and intercultural communication and can help tackle the challenge of intercultural education.

---

[40] Pierpaolo Donati, *Relational Sociology: A New Paradigm for the Social Sciences* (Routledge, 2012).

Broader Perspectives

While "relational paradigm" (RP) offers a robust framework for understanding social phenomena, relational interactionism does that and also challenges traditional sociological concepts and methods. This paradigm shift encourages social scientists to reconsider the boundaries and identities that emerge from relational networks, thus broadening the scope of socio-cultural inquiry.

"Relational interactionism" (RI) requires social scientists to make a paradigm-shift from a static view of social structure to a dynamic view of pattern and process of relational interaction of personal beings/Beings, leading to formation of relationship and emergence of social network. RI posits that society is constituted through relationships rather than merely through individual entities or groups. This approach encourages a critical examination of how social ties influence behavior, identity, and social change, integrating perspectives from relational realism and reflexivity. By focusing on the interconnectedness of social phenomena, RI offers a comprehensive framework for analyzing contemporary social issues, particularly in the intercultural context resulting from globalization.

RI is an approach that emphasizes the importance of understanding social phenomena as networks of relations rather than focusing solely on individual actors and actions, institutions and communities. It posits that social units and identities are not self-evident but emerge from specific contexts of relational interaction. This perspective shifts the analytical focus from subjects and objects to the relations and networks themselves, thereby altering how social boundaries and phenomena are conceptualized and theorized. It highlights the interconnectedness of social entities and the significance of boundaries in the study of social dynamics.

Theological Foundation of RICC

Apart from God's revelation, we cannot know God Himself (e.g. attributes of the Triune God), His work (e.g. creation and redemption) or His Word (both the "Incarnate Word" and the "inscripturated Word"). Communication stems from God's self-revelation, followed by a narrative inquiry into the pattern and process of Triune God's revelatory interaction with the created angelic and human beings within the context of the created order.

	FATHER	SON	HS
	Inspiration ("inscripturated" Word)		
	Visions, signs, dreams, oracular words recorded	Teaching & preaching recorded in Gospel books	Spirit of Jehovah & prophetic uttering (Heb 1:1)
	Incarnation (incarnate Word)		
	The Father's will & *Kenosis* (Phil 2)		HS upon virgin Mary (Mt 1:20)
	Illumination (knowing the inspired Word)		
	Sent by the Father (Jn 15:26)	Witnessed by HS (Jn 14:26, 15:26)	Illumination (1Cor 2:6-16; Jn 16:13)
	Resurrection		
	"But God raised him from the dead" (Acts 13:30)	"...and who through the Spirit of holiness was appointed the Son of God in power by his resurrection from the dead: *Jesus Christ our Lord.*" (Ro 1:4)	

DIACHRONIC ← development OT & NT

Figure 3. Dynamic Revelation of the Trinity

Trinitarian Paradigm of Relational Intercultural Communication[41]

Colin E. Gunton, in his volume, *The Promise of Trinitarian Theology*, makes a statement that is central to the purpose of this book: "Theology... is the enterprise of thought which seeks to express conceptually and as well as possible both the being of God and the implications of that being for human existence on earth."[42] The tying together of concept and practical implication are nowhere more necessary than they are in the study of communication.

---

[42] Colin E Gunton, *The Promise of Trinitarian Theology* (London: T&T Clark, 2003), 7.

Our question then becomes what we can learn about communication from the interaction of Father, Son, and Spirit. Secondly, we want to consider what those lessons of "intra-trinitarian interaction" (from within the Trinity) mean for our human communication vertically (i.e. personal Beings of the Triune God communicating with angelic/human beings within the created order) and horizontally (i.e. communication within the created order of angelic/human beings.)

Communicative Interaction within the Trinity

Insights about Communication between the Members of the Trinity

The Bible speaks of communication between Father, Son and Spirit in multiple ways and passages. We have chosen some for illustration, but the material suggested below is not at all exhaustive.

a. "Let us make man in our own image."

> The plural construction of this phrase from Genesis 1 and 2 permits (yet does not require) communicative interaction between members of the Trinity. Other possible readings would see the "us" as referring to the heavenly hosts who are present during creation, or perhaps as a plural which grammatically denotes majesty.[43] Still, for our purposes, the allusion to a dialog in the heavenlies which opens the door for a later full expression of the Triune nature of God is significant in our study of communication.

b. The Upper Room Discourse of John 13 – 17, especially John 17.

> The discourse of Jesus with His disciples gives us a rich view into dialog between the Son and the Father. There are numerous views into the communication between Father and Son in these chapters, but perhaps one of the best to demonstrate our point is found in John 17:8, "for I gave them the words you gave me and they accepted them. They knew with certainty that I came from you, and they believed that you sent me."[44]

c. Perichoresis

> Perichoresis is a theological term which describes mutual indwelling within the Trinity. Some authors suggest that even better than "indwelling" is the word, "interpenetration." At any rate, the concept calls us to acknowledge the nature of the relationship between the

---

[43] Genesis 1:26 translator's note 4 in the NET Bible, page 5. NET Bible, New English Translation; USA, Biblical Studies Press, 1996.
[44] John 17:8 New International Version

Members of the Trinity.[45] That relationship includes interactive communication at a far deeper level than mere words.

Insights about intercultural communication between humans

The interactive communication that we see within the Trinity points us toward insights into our own intercultural communication between humans.

In the first place, there is a mutual depth of understanding between Father, Son and Spirit. They are each perfectly known and they each perfectly know the other members of the Trinity.

Intercultural communication builds upon a foundation that all parties have in common. The example of interactive knowledge between the members of the Trinity points us toward a foundation of ever-increasing understanding of those we interact with as well – whether from our own culture or another. The point being that communication improves as interaction increases. (There is a caution here – the fact that communication improves does not necessarily mean that agreement increases.)

A second insight has to do with what exactly is shared between the Three. As we speak of interactive communication, this insight has to do with the nature and subject of that interaction. We will look at how Father, Son and Holy Spirit share their Being, goals, methods, results, process, and outcomes.

Shared Being

Father, Son and Spirit are each God, and yet each is distinct from the Other Two. John 17:21 is one of many places in the Bible where this truth is visible, "... that all of them may be one, Father, just as you are in me and I am in you. May they also be in us so that they world may believe that you have sent me."

The lessons for humanity are important to note here. Scripture teaches us that there are real differences between Father, Son and Spirit. The Three are distinct, and yet they are also unified by what they hold in common.

In the human realm, we also have both differences and similarities. We so easily focus on the differences that often we miss the unifying elements of our humanity. Unity recognizes the differences between cultures and yet builds on the unity of our shared humanity.

---

[45] Walter A. Elwell, ed., *Evangelical Dictionary of Theology*, Baker reference library (Grand Rapids, Mich.: Baker Book House, 1984), accessed January 31, 2025, https://covers.openlibrary.org/b/id/6623103-M.jpg. "Perichoresis" article by S.M Smith. Deeper treatment in terms of Trinitarian theology can be found in *The One, the Three, and the Many: God, Creation and the Culture of Modernity* by Colin E. Gunton: Cambridge, UK: Cambridge University Press, 8th printing 2004, pp 163-166.

Shared Goals
The Triune God has told us what He/They are doing: creating a New Heaven and New Earth (Rev 21) for example. He also is preparing a people for His own glory (Rev 7:9).

These shared goals include difficult moments. John 12:27 points to Jesus' troubled soul as He considered the cross. "... what shall I say? Father, save me from this hour? No, it was for this very reason I came to this hour." The Father and Son shared a goal that Jesus pursued even at great cost to Himself, and even with a troubled soul.

The lesson for humanity is that one thing that strengthens communication is a shared purpose. That shared purpose can sometimes be pleasant. But it is not necessarily true that a painful purpose will divide. People whose hearts are joined in unity around shared goals can endure difficulties in completing that common purpose.

Shared Methods
In John 5, Jesus explained that He, the Son, "can do nothing by himself, he can only do what he sees his Father doing, because whatever the Father does, the Son also does" (John 5:19).

Across Scripture we see Father, Son and Spirit working in unity toward their goals and using common methods; this is the case in Creation, in the history of Israel, in salvation, in giving us the Inspired Word of God. These shared methods are part of interactive communication within the Trinity.

Once again, lessons to humanity are not hard to see. Where humans share purpose and being but differ in method it is not long before interaction becomes strained. On the other hand, when people use common methods to attain common goals based on common human realities, those are the conditions that encourage interaction and communication.

Shared Results
The story of creation ends with an evaluation of the results: "God saw all that He had made, and it was very good" (Gen 1:31).

Jesus, in the Upper Room discourse, similarly talks with the Father about the shared results of the disciple-making that He did during the incarnation: "...I protected them and kept them safe by that name you gave me. None has been lost except the one doomed to destruction so that Scripture would be fulfilled" (John 17:12b). The purpose of preparing disciples had been set at the beginning. Later, approaching the end, Jesus comments on the shared results that all of the disciples had been protected.

There is once again a lesson for human intercultural communication. A strong encouragement for healthy communication is to continue interacting as results become visible. The idea of feedback is not simply human psychology. The shared results of shared endeavors, when discussed and noted together, become strong tools for ongoing interaction and communication.

Shared Process: love
Tracing the theme of "love" through the Bible, and especially the Gospel of John, leads us to realize that the process by which God works is a shared commitment to love. "For God so loved the world that He gave His one and only Son" (John 3:16); and "God is love" (1 John 4:8, 16) are two examples of this theme. The process by which God the Father, God the Son and God the Holy Spirit do their work is through love.

Unlike the other interactive communication ideas we have looked at, the idea that communication improves with a shared process is not sufficient in itself. This time the concept is a particular kind of shared process: it is shared process of love that is seen in the Trinity and by which They interact with One Another and with the World.

As humans who communicate, we are likewise called to an interactive process of love. John 13:35 tells us, in frank and clear language, that one key for evangelizing the world is mutual love among Christians, "By this everyone will know that you are my disciples, if you love one another."

One of the most powerful forms of communicating the Good News of our loving God is for His children to love one another. That call to mutual love crosses all economic and political barriers. It can be done without mastering new languages. It is part of the Great Commission that says, "go and make disciples of all nations" (Matthew 28:19) because the love that we show to others in the Family of God ends up being a testimony not just for the sake of the Church, but for "all men" (John 13:35).

In practical terms, the biblical concept of fellowship (*koinonia*) is a visible outworking of love. Biblical fellowship calls people together in a common love for God, a common love for one another, and a common experience in living a Christian life even under antagonistic conditions. "I want to know Christ... yes, to know the participation in his sufferings" (Philippians 3:10) points to Paul's desire to draw closer to Christ by sharing in His sufferings. That same word is used to describe the horizontal relationship between Christians in Acts 2:42-47. Fellowship in that early church illustration included shared activities like Bible study, meals, worship, and prayer. As time went on, the horizontal interactions in the early church also involved suffering together for the sake of Christ.

Hebrews 10:33 – 34 uses a form of the word "koinonia" to talk about shared suffering.[46]

In later portions of this book, we will discuss the transformative power of relationship as we see through progression from being (the ontological nature of a Creator or a created being) to belonging (the relationship patterns that we have called vertical and horizontal relational interaction), and becoming (the shaping that brings about transformative or transgressional change of character, beliefs or behaviors). Fellowship is a powerful force in that "belonging" level of change, as people interact with one another based on Christian relationships in all kinds of social and physical environments.

Love is also key to the vertical communication that we call "worship"; "love the Lord your God with all your heart and with all your soul and with all your mind" (Matthew 22:37 – 40).

Shared Outcome: Joy

There is one final way that the Father, Son and Spirit are united in mutual interaction. The outcome that all Three share, and that they share with Christians, is joy. It is a joy shared in the harmony of relationship and an individual joy that each one experiences.

The arrival of Jesus to this world was accompanied by the angelic promise that His birth would be "good news that will cause great joy for all the people" (Luke 2:10).

Jesus' willingness to be sacrificed was done with the outcome of joy in mind: Hebrews 12:2 tells us that it was "for the joy set before him he endured the cross, scorning its shame, and sat down at the right hand of the throne of God." The same theme, although with different words, is also seen in Hebrews 1:9 where we read that the Father has anointed "you with the oil of joy."

The Spirit of God is manifest in people through the demonstration of His characteristics, which include joy (Galatians 5:22).

The multiplied outcome of joy is perhaps most visible, though, in Matthew 25. The parable describes a man who entrusts his possessions to his household servants before leaving for a voyage. When he returns, some of those servants, knowing the heart of the master, gave back more than they had received. To those good and faithful servants, the repeated phrase is, "come and share in your master's happiness."

The Son enters the joy of the Father by building a Church that includes all tribes and tongues and nations (Rev. 7:9). The Son redeems the Church through His own suffering which He endured "for the joy set before Him."

---

[46] Colin Brown, *The New International Dictionary of New Testament Theology*, vol. 3 (Grand Rapids, Mich.: Zondervan, 1975).

The Spirit multiplies that joy into the hearts of Christians, described as the fruit of the Spirit. In that way, the outcome of communication between Father, Son and Spirit is joy which is to all nations through the Savior.

This section has considered the interactive communication that takes place between members of the Trinity, and the lessons that such communication has for us as human communicators. Tying together vertical and horizontal communication in light of the nature of our Triune God now leads us to develop more completely a Trinitarian Model of Communication. First we will look at communication between Father, Son and Spirit. Following that, we will go into more detail in vertical relational communication between the Creator and humankind.

Communication within the Trinity

Members of the Trinity communicate with One Another in a context of mutual service, not of self-service.

Thinking of the outcomes of any communication interaction, Trinitarian communication promotes the idea of seeking to serve the Other rather than focusing solely on self-interest. Philippians 2 ties the ideal "other-focus" of horizontal communication to the Trinity: "In your relationships with one another, have the same mindset as Christ Jesus: who being in very nature God did not consider equality with God something to be used to his own advantage; rather, he made himself nothing by taking the very nature of a servant, being made in human likeness" (Philippians 2:6,7).

Inter-Trinitarian communication rejoices at diversity.

The Bible is filled with pictures of diversity:

Creation has its amazing diversity of life forms which survive a wide range of physical environments.

Humanity displays a plethora of diversity in areas like language, cultural patterns, geographical preferences, and physical characteristics.

Within the Church there are diverse gifts (I Corinthians 12). Some preach, some teach, some care for the young or the aged, some are builders, etc.

In each of these areas of diversity, there is also a call for unity. I Corinthians 11:4, for example, points out the common Spirit that unifies the diversity of gifts. Revelation 7:9 points to the unity of humanity in worshipping Christ, even while simultaneously pointing to the diversity of languages, tribe, tongue and people.

A God who is Three and yet One forces our minds to accept the unity that exists in diversity. Father, Son and Spirit are distinct from one another. They are diverse. Yet they are all God, a unified One. This triunity points us toward a strong implication for communication: diversity is not antagonistic to communication. Diversity creates an occasion for finding unifying principles that join diverse Beings/beings together.

Inter-Trinitarian communication goes beyond words

The old adage that "actions speak louder than words" is true of God's communication within the Trinity. The concept of "perichoresis" speaks to an inter-animation that occurs between Father, Son and Spirit. Somewhat like the vertical relationship described as the indwelling of the Holy Spirit, the concept here is that the Three members of the Trinity are mutually involved, mutually in-dwelling One Another. One of the clearest expressions of this is found in the Upper Room Discourse in John 16 and 17. John 17:21 gives us a brief but powerful expression of "perichoresis." Jesus prays to the Father with these words, "that all of them may be one, Father, just as you are in me and I am in you..."

This inter-animation leads to a form of communication deeper than words alone. In John 12 we read the account of a voice from heaven that was audible and understandable to a multitude of people listening to Jesus' teaching. Jesus was foretelling His upcoming trip to Jerusalem and the suffering that would accompany that trip. As He finished this very public prayer, Jesus asked that the Father's Name be glorified. The Father's audible response was "I have glorified it and will glorify it again."

The multitude that was listening to Jesus began to speculate whose voice they had heard, and Jesus ended the conversation with these words, "This voice was for your benefit, not mine."

Within the Trinity, there is a deep understanding that includes words but also goes beyond words. There are times when the words used between the members of the Trinity are not to increase their own understanding, but for the benefit of created beings who hear.

Inter-Trinitarian communication is aimed at good goals

God is good (Psalm 100:5). The results and outcomes of His actions are good. The creation was pronounced "good" (Genesis 1:10, 12, 18, 25, 31). The Word He spoke at creation accomplished that which was good.

The Word of God is good. Psalm 119 seems to search for metaphors to show how good, how sweet, how powerful, and how influential the Word of God is; a light to our path, the joy of our hearts, the wisdom that surpasses the wisdom of the elders.

The Book of Hebrews tells us that the God who communicated through Scripture has, in these later times, also communicated through Jesus Christ (Hebrews 1:1-2). The goals that brought Jesus to take on human flesh and so become our Redeemer were good beyond our imagination.

Just briefly thinking of what Triune God does as He communicates is enough to point us toward an understanding of communication aimed at healthy, good goals. We are warned to let no "unwholesome talk" come from our mouths (Ephesians 4:29), but rather to speak so as to build up and benefit those who listen. The model of communication that we have in the Father, Son and Spirit is aimed at achieving good goals. Human, horizontal speech is to aim at those same good results.

The result of Inter-Trinitarian communication is *koinonia*, love, unity and glory.[47]

Paul, writing to his protégé Timothy, explains that his goal in teaching was "love, which comes from a pure heart and a good conscience and a sincere faith" (1 Timothy 1:5). Teaching, a sort of communication, in the Bible is aimed at good outcomes – at results of purity and good conscience and faith. Those results in human terms are only natural when we consider that it is a Good God who first communicated with us. That same God now uses His communication by Word, by Spirit, through creation, and through the Bible to encourage us, to edify, to unite and to bring glory to Himself. As we see those results of Trinitarian communication in Scripture we also see their relevance for our own communication.

Over the past several pages, we have looked at what the Bible teaches about communication within the Trinity and the implications that has for us in our horizontal communication. Now we want to specifically consider vertical communication: what does God do to communicate with humankind, and how does the Bible say we are to respond?

Communication between the Trinity and humankind (vertical)

Vertical communication is that which connects Creator Beings (Father, Son, Spirit) with created beings (angels, demons, humans). Any treatment of communication from a Relational Interactive perspective needs to bear in mind that horizontal experiences between people are not the only kinds of communication that exist. The following brief treatment will give some of the biblical foundations that help us to better see communication in vertical terms. The ideas below will move back and forth from Old Testament to New

---

[47] See Wan and Cloud, *Doxological Missiology*.

Testament but in either case, we see God communicating with His created beings.

God is Active in Communication

If we wish to create a model of intercultural communication that is accurate in the real world, we need to begin with a God who interacts with humanity through His presence and His message. The apparent power of horizontal communication is misleading; it misses the eternal and infinite nature of communication that includes both God and created beings. That Divine element of communication is one of the factors that led us to the RICC model.

There are many Scriptures that show how God is active in communication:

Genesis chapters 1 - 3 speak to the communication that took place seamlessly in the earliest days after Creation. God spoke to Adam and Eve (for instance, 1:28-30). God spoke to others in the Old Testament also, notably to Moses in several instances. When we think of God communicating with humankind, one clear example is that God Himself wrote the Ten Commandments onto the original stone tablets (Exodus 31:18).

Ephesians 4:3 tells us that as Christians we are to preserve unity, but it is a particular kind of unity: "being diligent to preserve the unity of the Spirit in the bond of peace." God, in His active involvement in our communication, calls us to a unity as people that is based on the unity of the Holy Spirit who indwells all His people.

Acts 2 tells the story of God's message being communicated well beyond the usual limits of human ability and yet still using human languages (Acts 2:1-11). At Pentecost, God gave people the ability to communicate in languages they did not know so that others who did speak those languages would hear of "the mighty deeds of God" (verse 11).

David Stevens captures the weight of what God did at Pentecost in his book, *God's New Humanity*.[48] He writes, ". . .apart from the supernatural, unifying work of God's Spirit, any attempt to live out our identity as God's New Humanity will prove futile. Only as we discover that reality of our oneness sourced in the Holy Spirit can we live out an authentic diversity in unity in the body of Christ. Such unity is a supernatural experience and can never be contrived or manufactured or organized by mere human effort. This is the message of Pentecost."[49]

---

[48] David E. Stevens, *God's New Humanity: A Biblical Theology of Multiethnicity for the Church* (Eugene, OR: Wipf and Stock Publishers, 2012).

[49] Stevens, *God's New Humanity: A Biblical Theology of Multiethnicity for the Church*, 121.

Tying Steven's concepts into our discussion of communication, we see God as active at supernaturally bringing about a level of communication that is both horizontal and vertical.

God's involvement in human communication is also seen in the biblical use of communication terms: Jesus is the Word of God in John 1. Hebrews chapter 1 tells us that God spoke through the prophets, but in these last days has spoken through His Son. First John 1:1 uses the vocabulary of communication to describe Jesus Christ as the ultimate communication: "That which was from the beginning, which we have heard, which we have seen with our eyes, which we have looked at and our hands have touched – this we proclaim concerning the Word of life." Jesus did not simply speak the Word; He was and is the fullness of communication that is pictured through the human analogy of language.

One final biblical passage speaks to God's involvement in human communication. Revelation 7:9 describes the multitude so great that no one could count them, praising the Lord as one united group that comes from "every nation, tribe, people and language" When God is involved in communication, even the differences bring unity and harmony. There is understanding regardless of the multitude of languages involved.

Vertical Communication Through Creation

The Old Testament tells us of God's communication through His creation. "The heavens declare the glory of God" (Psalm 19:1), is one example. The book of Job speaks to how God tells of His nature and His work by way of creation.

Paul picks up on this theme in Romans 1:20, "For since the creation of the world God's invisible qualities - His eternal power and divine nature - have been clearly seen, being understood from what has been made, so that people are without excuse."

We all recognize that horizontal communication takes place through objects. We speak of "status symbols" as a way that a person might boast of their position by way of their possessions and objects. Donald Smith,[50] in his "twelve languages of culture", includes "artifactual communication." We easily see how artifacts – things - are important parts in horizontal communication.

What we see in this vertical dimension is that God also communicates to humanity by way of objects that He made. The stars, the earth, the animal world are all speaking of the glory of God to those who have ears to hear.

---

[50] Donald K. Smith, *Creating Understanding,* 2nd edition. (Artists in Christian Testimony International LLC, 2022), 304.

Vertical Communication Through Relationship

When we think of all the possible relational forms that God could choose to model for humanity, and all the possible forms that He could use to communicate His desired forms of interaction with people, it is notable that He often chooses the family. The fact that God the Father and God the Son invite people to become the children of God is one of those phrases that we use so often that it loses its power. But the power is there.

Dennis Kinlaw, in his work, *Let's Start with Jesus*[51], goes so far as to suggest that the family context is not an accommodation to human thought patterns, but in fact is the basic form of the Trinity. Kinlaw's suggestion is that when God created the human family, He modeled it after His own Trinitarian relationships. The idea that we are created in God's image, in this way, includes the fact of human family structures.

This family context is communicated through Scripture in many ways. The names used for the Father and the Son certainly apply. The intimacy seen in the prayers of Jesus, especially John 17, are familial. The parables that Jesus used to help describe the Kingdom of God are also familial, with stories like the prodigal son and the rich young ruler being used to teach Kingdom truth with words used for family.

Vertical Communication Through Scripture

When we think of how God communicates with created beings through Scripture, there are two very distinct ideas. First, we have the declarations in Scripture that are God-breathed truths intended to communicate to humans. Secondly, we find the narratives through which God's story, also God-breathed, reveals divine characteristics through the narratives of His actions and words.

Starting with the declarations, we can think of passages like Josua 1:8, "Keep this Book of the Law always on your lips; meditate on it day and night, so that you may be careful to do everything written in it."

The virtues of the Word of God are highlighted in Psalm 1 as well, which tells us that God has communicated through His Word and there are benefits and blessings for those who delight themselves in that Word.

The Psalms contain many passages that speak to the value of God's Word as a guiding light to people (Psalm 119:105).

The prophet Isaiah wrote in a time of distress and turmoil for the people of Israel. In that time of uncertainty, God declares the faithfulness of His Word as that which is trustworthy when all else fails. In Isaiah 40:6b-8 for example, we read "all people are like grass, and all their faithfulness is like

---

[51] Dennis F. Kinlaw, *Let's Start with Jesus: A New Way of Doing Theology* (Grand Rapids, Mich: Zondervan Academic, 2005), 24–28.

the flowers of the field. The grass withers and the flowers fall, because the breath of the Lord blows on them. Surely the people are grass. The grass withers and the flowers fall, but the word of our God endures forever."

Moving to the New Testament, Jesus calls wise those who respond to the Word that He spoke: "Therefore everyone who hears these words of mine and puts them into practice is like a wise man who built his house on the rock. The rain came down, the streams rose, and the winds blew and beat against that house; yet it did not fall, because it had its foundation on the rock. But everyone who hears these words of mine and does not put them into practice is like a foolish man who built his house on sand. The rain came down, the streams rose, and the winds blew and beat against that house, and it fell with a great crash." (Matthew 7:24-27).

John wrote his Gospel with a particular communicative intent. We read in John 20:30-31, "Jesus performed many other signs in the presence of his disciples, which are not recorded in this book. But these are written that you may believe that Jesus is the Messiah, the Son of God, and that by believing you may have life in his name."

Paul's writing to Timothy is another example of Scripture that tells us that it is meant to be understood as God's communication to people. 2 Timothy 3:16 tells us plainly, "All Scripture is God-breathed and is useful for teaching, rebuking, correcting and training in righteousness, so that the servant of God may be thoroughly equipped for every good work."

Interestingly the Bible also alludes to the impact of vertical communication upon non-human created beings. Angels and demons are aware of the declarations and narratives of Scripture and they, too, recognize God's vertical communication. Peter, writing about the Messianic prophesies in the Old Testament, tells us, "Even angels long to look into these things" (1 Peter 1:12). In a similar way, James 2:19 tells us that the demons shudder when they realize that the communication of God was meant to stir up both faith and works in humans.

Communication through Scripture includes narratives that tell stories of God and His acts among people as a way of teaching the truths He wants us to understand. The book of Acts is a long report on the investigation made by Luke into the way that God worked in the first days of the fledging church. Acts 1 ties that investigative report to the idea of communication from God to man. Christ's teaching after the resurrection and before the ascension is said to have focused on "speaking about the kingdom of God," (Acts 1:1-3).

Other narrative teachings of Scripture can be found in Hebrews 11. That chapter uses a multitude of examples from the Old Testament to show how the stories of those faithful men and women have been given to us in Scripture as a means of interacting with God: "And without faith it is impossible to please God, because anyone who comes to him must believe that he exists and that he rewards those who earnestly seek him." (Hebrews 11:6). Vertical communication requires both a God who speaks and people who respond in faith. The chapter continues with story after story of Old Testament heroes who lived their lives believing the promises of God. They responded with faith to the vertical communication God had directed to them.

First Corinthians 15:1-11 gives us another narrative which tells us about communicating the nature of God. Summarizing the content of the apostles' preaching, Paul highlights Jesus' life, death and resurrection. Twice in these few verses, Paul emphasizes that this set of facts about the life of Christ were the content of his preaching (verse 1 – "the gospel I preached to you" and verse 11 – "this is what we preached, and this is what you believed"). The narratives of the cross, the empty tomb, the post-resurrection appearances and the ascension are stories that God uses to open hearts ("what you believed") and tell the story of redemption.

There is another way that God has spoken in Scripture. The Bible records several theophanies; passages in which a pre-incarnate Christ is present at some particular moment in the lives of His people. Daniel 3 tells the story of a confused king Nebuchadnezzar who threw three men (Hananiah, Mishael and Azariah by their Hebrew names; Shadrack, Meshach and Abed-nego by their Babylonian names) into the blazing fire of a furnace for their refusal to worship his gods. As he looked into the flames, though, he asked his servants, "Weren't there three men that we tied up and threw into the fire?" The servants assure the king that yes, there were three men. "Look! I see four men walking around in the fire unbound and unharmed, and the fourth looks like a son of the gods" (Daniel 3:24-25). The communication within this theophany is understood instantly by the king. He recognizes the power of the God of Shadrach, Meshach and Abed-nego (3:28) and makes it a criminal offense to "say anything against the God of Shadrach, Meshach and Abed-nego."

God also communicates with His creation by way of miracles. There are numerous places in the Bible where prophets or the Lord Jesus did miracles. Perhaps one of the clearest, as far as its communication purpose, is found in Mark 2. A paralytic was brought to Jesus, who then announced that the man's sins were forgiven (Mark 2:5). Religious leaders of the day, scribes and pharisees, understood these words to be blasphemous. "Who can forgive sins but God alone?" they reasoned (Mark 2:7). This was exactly the lesson that Jesus was seeking to communicate – that He is God. And so He then asks, "which is easier: to say to this paralyzed man, "your sins are forgiven," or to say, "Get up, take your mat and walk? But I want you to know that the Son of

Man has authority on earth to forgive sins." So he said to the man, I"I tell you, get up, take your mat and go home."

The paralytic rose and picked up his mat. The miraculous healing communicated Jesus' desired message.

Jesus not only did miracles. He used those miracles to communicate truths in a way that went far beyond simple words. In the Mark 2 story, we see Jesus using a miracle to show His authority to forgive sins. In other places He used miracles to communicate His authority over death (for example with Lazarus in John 11:43 – 45). In the case of the miracle of raising Lazarus, "many of the Jews. . .who had seen what Jesus did, believed in Him." Others, of course, did not and began looking for a way to have Him executed. Nevertheless, the miracle had its power in communicating the authority of Christ over death, and in communicating the truthfulness of His Kingdom teaching.

The New Testament gives us specific insights into communication that could not have been possible before that. Specifically, the New Testament speaks of God's communication through vertical, cross-cultural revelation through the incarnation of Jesus Christ, the inspiration of the Scriptures, and the illumination of believers as they grow in understanding.

Those three processes speak to moments when communication flows from theo-culture to human-culture; a form of cross-cultural communication. The processes in each case begin with God's intention to make Himself known.

Inspiration

We have already seen many ways that God has communicated via the Bible. When we speak of inspiration, we specifically consider the process by which God gave us the Bible. The Greek word that was used to describe this process, translated into English as "inspired," literally means "God-breathed" (2 Timothy 3:16). "All Scripture is God-breathed and is useful for teaching, rebuking, correcting and training in righteousness."

This God-breathed Word captures precisely the intended meaning of God, "explaining spiritual realities with Spirit-taught words" (1 Cor. 2:13) Peter adds more to this concept of Inspiration by telling us that the process was initiated by God. "For prophecy never had its origin in the human will, but prophets, though human, spoke from God as they were carried along by the Holy Spirit" (2 Peter 1:21).

These three passages point us toward a process of inspiration that includes human agents receiving God's thoughts and writing them under His direction, and solely at His pleasure. This form of vertical communication was initiated and overseen by God in all ways; and yet people were involved in taking those thoughts and then, led by the Spirit, putting them into appropriate human words.

Incarnation

Hebrews 1 tells us that the incarnation of Jesus Christ was done as a means of speaking to humanity (Hebrews 1:2). Through the God-man Jesus, God has communicated, "the radiance of God's glory and the exact representation of his being, sustaining all things by his powerful word."

John 1 gives us a similar lesson, telling us that Jesus has been from the beginning. John traces the involvement of Jesus in creation and later as the Incarnate Son of God. He was the light of men, and in Him was life (John 1:4). That Word of God became flesh (the incarnation) and as John says, "we have seen his glory." (John 1:14). The message that was communicated through the incarnation is given in this passage: "For the Law was given through Moses; grace and truth came through Jesus Christ. No one has ever seen God, but the one and only Son, who is himself God and in closest relationship with the Father, has made him known." (John 1: 17-18).

Of course, there is more to the incarnation than God explaining God. The incarnation also allowed for the sacrificial death of Christ as atonement for sin. There was more than just communication in Jesus' humanity. Still the fact that the incarnation fulfilled several purposes does not minimize the important role it played in communicating about God to mankind.

Continuing with other truths that were communicated by the incarnation, we learn in Scripture how the Son interacts with the Father. Reading through all of the Gospels we see Jesus submitting to the will of the Father. Perhaps the most striking of these statements is in Luke 22:42 where Jesus prays to the Father that the trial of the cross might be avoided, "yet now my will, but yours be done". The Gospel of John picks up another nuance of that story, too, relating that when the soldiers came to arrest Jesus, some of His followers began to offer physical resistance. Jesus' response to Simon Peter's protective gesture is found in John 18:11. "Put your sword away! Shall I not drink the cup the Father has given me?" The incarnation gives us glimpses into the interactions between the incarnate Christ and the Father; lessons that communicate to us about the nature of the Trinity.

Philippians 2 takes the lessons of submission and humility by the incarnate Christ one step further, making it a model that we also ought to follow. Paul calls us to "have the same mindset as Christ Jesus; Who, being in very nature God, did not consider equality with God something to be used to his own advantage; rather, he made himself nothing by taking the very nature of a servant " (Philippians 2:5-6). This famous *kenosis* passage communicates with us the importance of a humble attitude based on the example of the humility of Christ.

Illumination

Interactive communication between Triune God and humanity includes illumination of the believer as well as the incarnation that we have now considered. Regarding illumination, we speak of the Spirit's role in opening human understanding of the things that we read in Scripture.

Acts 16:14 is a subtle yet powerful narrative example of this illumination process. Paul had been preaching the gospel to the folks of Philippi. A woman named Lydia heard that gospel communication as Paul explained and taught it. Verse 14 tells us that "The Lord opened her heart to respond to the things spoken by Paul."

We can see that in some areas of communication, there is both a need for preaching/teaching by gifted people AND a need for the Spirit of God to open hearts. The illumination of believers so that they understand the message they have heard is a significant element in communication of spiritual truth. The Spirit opens the heart to believe what has been preached.

Ephesians 1 helps us to see how the illumination of the believer is a part of God's communication. Ephesians 1:13 tells us that "after listening to the message of truth, the gospel of your salvation – having also believed you were sealed in Him with the Holy Spirit of promise." The communication of the message of the gospel leads to the personal involvement of the Holy Spirit in sealing the believer.

Like a chain of blessings that flow from that original "listening to the message," Ephesians 1 continues with Paul's written prayer that God would give to the Ephesians "a spirit of wisdom and of revelation in the knowledge of Him, that the eyes of your heart may be enlightened" (Eph 1:17-18).

The point is that just as vertical communication includes the inspiration of the written Word of God and the incarnation of the Son of God, so too it includes that illumination of opening the heart of the believer to understand and to believe.

This is a very practical point for us. The communication of God's Word is never a purely human matter. We are involved – that is why we have passages like Matthew 28:18 – 20 that tell us to go and proclaim the gospel. But Gospel advance is never a matter of strictly human strategy and communication ability. We as humans are called to go and to preach. God is the One who opens hearts to believe. Gospel communication needs to be aware of this and approach the ministry of the Word with humility and dependence on the power, leading, wisdom, and illumination of the Spirit in making His name known.

Vertical Communication through Redemption and a Transformed Life

God's revelation of Himself and His nature goes well beyond simple words. His actions also serve to communicate His character and His grace. Of special interest is the mercy that He has shown to humanity by making a way of salvation possible. First Peter 1:12 gives us a picture into how God communicates with angels: He instructs them about Himself by allowing them to see human redemption. "Things into which angels long to look" tells us that as God works out His redemptive plan on earth, there are created beings called angels who are also learning from that communication.

Vertical Communication in Other Means

Daniel Villa, in his chapter in *Case Studies in Christian Communication in an Asian Context*[52], mentions other ways that the Bible shows God in communication with humankind:

- Through the analogy of human body parts, such as face, hands or eyes (for example, Isaiah 64:2 and Psalm 34:15).
- God's involvement in history, for instance regarding the Babylonian captivity (Jeremiah 50:1-16).
- God's revelation of His nature through the Old Testament calendar and religious observation (Leviticus 23:15-16).
- The Church, according to 1 Peter 2:9, is a holy nation, God's own people, chosen to proclaim.

Results of Communication by God

When God communicates with people, there are results. Below we consider a few outcomes of vertical communication that can be seen in Scripture, specifically in John 17, the High Priestly prayer that Jesus lifted to the Father just a few hours before He went to the cross.

Joy

"...I say these things while I am still in the world, so that they may have the full measure of my joy within them." 17:13

Sanctification

Jesus prayed that the Father would, "sanctify them by the truth. Your word is truth." 17:17

---

[52] Ross W James, ed., *Case Studies in Christian Communication in an Asian Context* (Mandaluyong, Philippines: OMF Literature, Inc., 1989), 1–15.

Purpose

Jesus' prayer, spoken to the Father, was that "as you sent me into the world, I have sent them into the world" 17:18.

Unity

"that all of them may be one, Father, just as you are in me and I am in you." 17:21 and "I (Jesus) in them and you (the Father) in me so that they may be brought to complete unity" 17:23.

To see the Glory of the Son

"Father, I want those you have given me to be with me where I am, and to see my glory, the glory you have given me because you loved me before the creation of the world" 17:24.

Perfect/mature us

"I in them (speaking of those who believe in Christ), and Thou in Me, that they may be perfected in unity, that the world may know that Thou didst send Me, and didst love them even as Thou didst love Me." 17:23 (New American Standard Bible translation)

In horizontal communication, we look for behavioral responses to a message. An ad agency looks for increased sales of their client's product, or a not-for-profit organization measures the number of people on its mailing list. Communication about a political election seeks votes in favor of a particular candidate or political question.

Those human, horizontal communication examples remind us of the limitations that we as people have in communicating with one another. We can appeal for a change of emotional response. We can ask for behavioral responses. We can test to see if knowledge and information was received. Communication in human terms, in fact, parallels Bloom's triad of educational learning objectives: cognitive, affective and psychomotor. Human communication seeks to instill or impart knowledge, emotional, or behavioral responses, and to elicit responses accordingly.[53]

Where God is active in the communication, though, there are numerous other avenues for expression and for reception. The results of God's communication in areas seen in John 17 (joy, sanctification, purpose, unity, glory and ongoing maturation) are different from simply "knowing, being,

---

[53] James, ed., *Case Studies in Christian Communication in an Asian Context*, 6.

and doing." God's Word has a distinct ability to have impact beyond all we can ask or think.

Vertical Communication: Humanity's Communication to God

So far we have considered vertical communication from God to people. But like any healthy interactive relational communication, there are ways that people can interact and communicate with God. We close this vertical communication section with a few examples of how people also are involved in vertical communication.

Prayer

Prayer is a means of vertical communication between people and God. The Lord's Prayer in Matthew 6:9-13 gives us insight into this provision for direct communication. The provision of prayer for bringing our needs and concerns into God's presence is a strong tool for dealing with the anxiety and worries of life. Philippians 4:6-7 promises that communicating with God by prayer and supplication with thanksgiving is the antidote to anxiety. The result of that upward communication is peace, a guarded mind, and a guarded heart.

Vertical communication has an impact that goes beyond any similarity to horizontal communication. We might ask a person for help, and they may be as involved as humanly possible. But they are not able to work in our hearts to bring peace or tranquility of thought and emotion. God's responses to the communication that He has made available is beyond human measure, as is the peace that He offers which "transcends all understanding" (Philippians 4:7.)

Faithfulness

Matthew 25 tells the story of a faithful steward. By modeling faithfulness in our lives and ministries, we communicate our heart's intention to God. The beauty is that this faithfulness is noticed. Verse 23 of that chapter reminds us of the Lord's reply, "well done, good and faithful servant. You have been faithful with a few things. I will put you in charge of many things. Come and share your master's happiness."

Seeking Him

Matthew 6:32-33 tells us that the Father is aware of our physical needs, and when we seek His kingdom and His righteousness, "all these things will be given to you as well." The amazing truth here is not only a God who supplies, but a God who responds to our seeking for Him by supplying. Just the search itself is part of our vertical communication.

Worship

Another area of vertical communication that is available to the Christian is in the area of worship. This worship can take on the shape of "psalms and hymns and songs of the Spirit." (Ephesians 5:19). This passage points to both horizontal communication (speaking to one another) and vertical communication to the Lord (sing and make music in your heart to the Lord).

Worship can be corporate communication to God, where many believers are united in their vertical communication with Triune God. Likewise, there are private, individual forms of worship that include simple personal holiness of life and avoidance of contamination with sin – the "true and proper worship" that Paul addresses in Romans 12:1-2.

Growing/Maturing

Finally, growth in our relationship with God and our knowledge of Him are also communication paths that we can use to show God that we are serious about walking with Him. 2 Peter 3:18 calls us to "grow in the grace and the knowledge of our Lord and Savior Jesus Christ." The fact that we are growing is itself a form of communication. Matthew 21:27-32 tells the story of a man who told his two sons to go to work in the vineyard. The first son said yes, but didn't go. The second son said no, but then regretted that decision, repented, and did go. Jesus concludes the story by calling on His audience (the chief priests of the temple in Jerusalem) to likewise repent.

Our communication with God is not limited to words. Our response to His Word, our actions of obedience and of growth, are also a means of vertical communication.

Summary

Over the past several sections, we have focused on theological perspectives on communication. The normal approach to communication is to limit it to horizontal relationships, or at best to assume that God uses the same communication tools for His own communication.

What we have seen, though, is that communication in vertical terms is broader than what we find in horizontal terms. God can and does communicate His thoughts and intentions well beyond the limitations of human communication channels. God can interact directly with the heart of the hearer, for example. Furthermore, He knows our human thoughts by way of prayers and intentions of our hearts that would not necessarily be available through normal human, horizontal communication.

The importance of interaction in the communication process has been noted throughout this section. We stress the interactive nature of both horizontal and vertical communication as a corrective to the common view of communication as a transaction between two static, stable Beings/beings. What we have seen is that there may be changes in positions as communication takes place. The nature of the Beings/beings does not necessarily shift (especially true with God. Consider the description of Jesus Christ who is the same yesterday, today and forever Hebrews 13:8), but the nature of the relationship can and does change. We have passed from darkness to light, from death to life. That change in us, through God's grace, brings about a change in how He interacts vertically with us.

Narrative Account of RICC & the Gospel (Jews + Gentile)

In the Book of Acts, there are several cross-cultural encounters that can help us to continue to build our model of relational interactive communication. In Figure 4 (below) we diagrammatically analyze the biblical story of Paul and Cornelius (Acts 10 and Acts 15). This is a helpful case study, showing communication elements in both monocultural and cross-cultural settings. In the figure, the letter V is used to identify matters of vertical communication, and H is used to identify horizontal communication. The value of this analysis is that it shows several ways that intercultural communication can be viewed:

- Through the lens of exclusion (for example from a Jewish dietary law perspective).
- Through the lens of gospel inclusion (a gospel for every tribe, tongue, nation and people).
- Through the lens of personal involvement (Peter or Cornelius individually, for example)
- Through the lens of collective involvement (the household of Cornelius and the national background of Peter).

The process of making the gospel known to Cornelius and then open to other Gentile communities required several steps of communication. Within the biblical text, we see people, God and angels all involved. We also see created beings increasing in their knowledge of Triune God and His character as the interactive, dynamic process develops.

This figure also helps us to see some of the dynamics involved in cross-cultural conflict. In the Acts 10 and 15 example, there was definite cross-cultural conflict as Jewish and Gentile-background believers had to understand one another in light of Old Testament practice and the newer revelation of God's actions in His Church. The overall goal of gospel advance, to go into all the world and preach the gospel, foreshadowed the need for clarifying just how Old Testament Judaism would fit within the New

Testament period. The interactions between Peter and Cornelius give us clarity on specific areas of friction that they needed to resolve. Many of those same areas of clarity are also needed for today's intercultural and cross-cultural Christian interactions.

	Level	Cornelius	Angel	Peter	Location
P R O C E S S	**P E R S O N A L** Acts 10	-God-fearing (V) & charity (H) 10:2 -Memorial offering (V) 10:4 -Sent 3 to invite -Family gathering -Filled with Spirit and with praise -teaches household to be baptized 10:24-48	-met and instructed Cornelius 10:2-6 (V & H)	-Lodging at Simon the tanner's house (gentile with unclean profession) -Vision & instruction 10:9-16 (V & H) -Invitation came 10:17-22 -Preached at Cornelius family gathering & realized God's impartiality. Acknowledged the work of the Spirit among Gentile audience. Baptized them 10:24-48	**C E S A R I A** (Acts 10)
	C O L L E C T I V E	Intercultural conflict between Jews & Gentiles surfaced at the house meeting, instructed by angel and initiated by Cornelius	-Angel's appearance and instruction 11:13-14	-intercultural conflict caused confrontation with resolution – 11:1-18 (informal gathering). -circumcised believers criticized Peter for breaking the law of separation and purity – **Jewish exclusion** -Peter's recounting of vision/invitation/house meeting with Cornelius as witnessed by 6 companions. -gentile household filled by Spirit and baptized by Spirit -conflict resolution – **Gospel inclusion** at the	**J E R U S A L E M**

| | | | | Jerusalem council 15:1-41 (formal council).
-mark of separation was previously circumcision 15:1-2
-OT: Prophets (15) and Moses (15)
-Paul and Barnabus shared the news of gentile conversion in Phonecia and Samaria 15:3.
-Paul addressed the council with "Gospel of Inclusion" because of the Lord's grace 15:7-11
-Triune God: God (4,8,13,14), HS (8), Jesus Christ (11) (V)
-James addressed the council (13-21)
-expansion to other cities (Antioch, Pamphylia etc.)
-intercultural clarification brought by delegates (22-29) Message of Gospel of inclusion well received in Antioch, Pamphylia, Cyrus, Syria, Cilicia (15:22-41). | |

Figure 4. Narrative Account of RICC and the Gospel to Jews & Gentile

Horizontal Communication

At this point, we move from communication within the Trinity and vertical communication to a more in-depth look at communication between people (horizontal communication). For the sake of the discussion in this book, we will limit our discussion to horizontal communication between Christian people. We do this in recognition of the indwelling Spirit in the lives of believers, and also because of the Christian's recognition of the authority of the Word of God, the Bible.

In the first place, communication between people can encourage toward godliness or it can encourage toward ungodly behavior. We will use the term "transformational" to describe communication that encourages godly growth. We will use the term, "transgressional" to speak of communication that promotes ungodliness.

Another point that arises when we speak of horizontal communication is the fact that, as humans, we use words to both reveal and to conceal. The parables of Jesus are an excellent example of His use of communication to make Kingdom truth available to those who wished to understand it, and yet to keep it hidden from those who were not volitionally directed toward those truths. In Mark 4:11-12 we read, "The secret of the kingdom of God has been given to you. But to those on the outside everything is said in parables so that they may be ever seeing but never perceiving, and ever hearing but never understanding; otherwise they might turn and be forgiven!"

In cross cultural situations that involve multiple languages, there are often moments when a speaker has the option of choosing speech patterns that will be understood by non-native speakers. A native speaker may choose vocabulary and grammar that is easy to understand, or that which is more complicated. Even though this is not a reference to parables, it is another way that horizontal communication can be both revealing and concealing, depending on the speaker, the topic, and the audience.

Human to human, horizontal communication will naturally fall into one of two categories regarding its intended outcomes. Some communication seeks the well-being of the hearer. Other communication is focused on the well-being of the speaker. Below are some brief notes about those two end-points for communication.

Communication that seeks the wellbeing of the hearer:

1 Corinthians 13, the Love Chapter of the Bible, is a call to put others before oneself.

Philippians 2:3-4 calls us to "Do nothing out of selfish ambition or vain conceit. Rather, in humility value others above yourselves, not looking to your own interests but each of you to the interests of the others."

Ephesians 4:29 reminds us to forego unwholesome talk, and instead to choose communication that will be good for building others up and that will give grace to hearers.

Ephesians 5:4 tells us to avoid silliness and course speech, but rather to focus on the giving of thanks.

Communicating the Gospel and encouraging transformational talk is also for the wellbeing of the hearer. Witnessing of our faith, even to the point of suffering or death, is a form of communication that is done for the wellbeing of those who watch/listen.

Communication that seeks the wellbeing of the speaker:

When self-serving communication is vertical, it can be a form of idolatry which objectifies God so that we conceive of Him as simply fulfilling our wishes.

A different attitude toward vertical communication can also be for one's own benefit, but in a transformational way. "Come now and let us reason together," says the Lord. "Though your sins are like scarlet, they shall be as white as snow; though they are red as crimson, they shall be like wool. If you are willing and obedient, you will eat the good things of the land; but if you resist and rebel, you will be devoured by the sword" (Isaiah 1:18-20) is a call to wisdom to benefit oneself, done in conjunction and in agreement with God and His ways.

The attitudinal difference between self-benefit that is transformational and self-interest that is transgressional has to do with the level of relational interaction involved. If the attitude is independence and a selfish desire for God to meet one's own needs, it is transgressional. But if there is a relationship that seeks to honor God and receive from Him the good gifts that He has offered, then there is a level of self-interest that is healthy and transformational.

When self-focused communication is horizontal, it also can move toward either transformational or transgressional. The transgressional form of self-serving is the objectification of the other people involved, as if the other person is expected to accomplish your whims and preferences. It is not an attitude that has relational interest in the other person, but only in what that person can do for you.

Transformational self-benefit is done in conjunction with the other person. This is the coach who wants to see his team do well both for the sake of his own career and for the sake of the players. This is the teacher who takes great joy at seeing her students excel. This is Paul who says, "make my joy complete by being like-minded" (Philippians 2:2). Was the unity of the Philippians for their good? Of course it benefited them. It also served Paul's interests so he could appeal to them with that self-benefit motivation (make my joy complete).

The relational attitude is what distinguishes self-interested communication that is transgressional from that which is transformational. When self-interest is the focus of communication, the question is whether that is in a healthy relationship to other people, or independent of others. When self-focus is done with an eye on the benefit to others as well, it can be a healthy sort of communication. But we will use the term, "worldly communication" to speak of self-focused communication that does not seek the best for others.

Figure 5 is a comparison of worldly, self-focused, independent communication compared to Trinitarian communication which seeks the best for all involved.

Communication type / Element	Worldly Communication	Trinitarian Communication
Biblical root	Tower of Babel- communication between people led them to be able to do anything. Technique and methodology has the appearance of strength and wisdom but can be a root of evil and destruction	Revelation 7 – every tribe and tongue and nation and people worship Revelation 28 all tears are dried
Goal	serve self, though possibly with a pretext of serving other.	Serve God and serve neighbors
Method	Polished, mechanical communication. Well designed. Calculating. Objectifying. Truth is not a strong virtue; lying is OK	Let no unwholesome talk come out of your mouth Edify one another
Result	Chaos	Love, unity
Process	Objectify people, slavery, misogyny, stereotype, all of the "isms"	Know and be known. Speak truth one to another. Let your yes be yes.
Metrics	Morality, attendance, sales	godliness
Source of Power	Human wisdom – James 3	Divine wisdom James 3

Figure 5. Comparison/contrast between worldly and Trinitarian communication patterns

On the left-hand side is worldly communication: mechanistic and self-interested. It will have the appearance of power. The right column shows the dynamic/interactive trinitarian relational approach. Within the heart of those communication approaches we see progress toward transformation or transgression.

If communication is based on trinitarian relational thought, then vertically it will know and be known by Triune God. Horizontally it will cause us to speak truth, to love one another, to let no unwholesome word come out of our mouth. Trinitarian communication will put the needs of the other person ahead of our own needs. Trinitarian communication will seek to build relational unity between those involved.

On the other hand, an independent mindset will communicate in ways to gain benefit for oneself without giving thought to the others involved.

Summary

We have looked at three distinct communication settings: 1) between Members of the Triune God, 2) vertically between God and humanity, and 3) between people in horizontal communication.

Those three distinct perspectives give us three very different approaches to communication, depending on the Beings/beings who are involved. Each of the three frames (within the Triune God, vertically between Creator and created, and horizontally across humanity) are real parts of communication. Standard approaches to communication focus on horizontal communication at the neglect of any vertical or inter-Trinitarian consideration. In this chapter we have tried to open the discussion so that communication is seen as a dynamic, interactive process either within a given cultural group, or across cultural groups including crossing between Triune God, angels, demons, and people.

CHAPTER 4
The Relational Interactionist Communication (RICC) Approach

The Relational Interactionist Communication (RICC) approach that we present in this volume stands out in three ways from current models or schools of thought:

1. The RICC model is aware of the individuals involved (the beings or Beings[54]) AND it is aware of the interaction between them. It describes a "both/and" state that allows us to have meaningful discussion about cultural habits, personality and individual characteristics AND also consider specific interactions formed by relationships between those beings/Beings.
2. The RICC model includes both horizontal and vertical communication. God the Father, Son and Spirit are interactively involved with people: they can, and do, interact with individual people and with groups of people. There is never just a human dyad in terms of communication. God is always present between any two people. He opens and closes our ability to understand and to be understood in our interactions.
3. The RICC model recognizes the central importance of volition. People "hear" when they are open to new input. Communication includes both a horizontal and a vertical volitional decision.

With these background ideas, we propose that communication be defined as:

Communication is the process between two or more beings/Beings of creating and interpreting messages that seek to elicit a response, and which include both horizontal and vertical interactions.[55]

From the above definition of communication, we can develop a definition of "intercultural communication":

Intercultural Communication is the process between two or more beings/Beings of creating and interpreting messages that seek to elicit a response, and which include both horizontal and vertical interactions that cross from one set of cultural patterns to another.

---

[54] The word "beings" referring to created entities like people, angels, demons, and animals. Beings (capitalized) refers to Father, Son, and/or Spirit – Divine Creator Beings.

[55] Adapted from Em Griffin *et al.*, page 6

Our model goes one step further, also giving us a definition of Relational Intercultural Communication:

Relational Intercultural Communication is the <u>relational</u> process between two or more beings/Beings of creating and interpreting messages that seek to elicit a response, and which include both horizontal and vertical interactions that occur between the varied patterns of life displayed by members of different cultural groups.

Introducing the Paradigm of Relational Intercultural Communication (RICC)

We are now moving into the Relational Intercultural Communication model. This model builds on the strengths of typical communication concepts, and yet it also includes insights from the relational interactionist approach. The remainder of this chapter will present and explain this RICC model.

RICC: A Brief Introduction

Relational Intercultural Communication is shown graphically in Figures 6 and 7.

Communi-cation Phase	Perception	Conception	Volition	Expression
Process	What we sense by human sensory perception	What we understand	What we decide	What we express

Communi-cation Phase	Perception	Conception	Volition	Expression
God's involvement Vertical Influence	"He who has ears to hear, let him hear." (Mt 11:15)	God opens hearts and minds (Acts 16:14, Luke 24:45-53)	-God works in you to will and to act according to His good purpose. (Phil 2:12 – 13) -transgressional volition by Satan "I will ascend, raise my throne" and other expressions of prideful will (Isaiah 14:13-14)	"May these words of my mouth and this meditation of my heart be pleasing in your sight." Psalm 19:14
Location	Process of external stimuli being filtered by internal	Internal process of growing to understand what was perceived	Personal beings respond to others and to the environment on the basis of decision	External process of expressing shaped by internal understanding

Communi-cation Phase	Perception	Conception	Volition	Expression
Communication factors	-Physical acuity (eyes, ears) -Media -Language (including register) -Previous experience -Personality gifting/ emotional state/emotional health -Context -Cultural norms -Self-perception -Heart habits: grace? Judgment?	- Worldview - Context - Previous experience - Relational factors - Cultural norms - Emotional state and emotional patterns -Relational posture toward other person like/dislike open/closed-Curiosity -Self-perception	-Communication can <u>motivate</u> toward godly decision "I urge you in view of God's mercy" Romans 12:1-3 -Communication can <u>invite</u> toward godly relationship: "Come to Me all you who are weary and burdened" (Matthew 11:28-29) -Communication can <u>describe</u> a better option I Cor 12:30-13:13 "Eagerly desire the greater gifts" is followed by description of love.	-Language spoken -Language level (register) -Previous experience -Personality, gifting -Language ability -Level of interpersonal knowledge -Emotional state -Context -Self and group perception

Figure 6. Interactive Relational Intercultural Communication

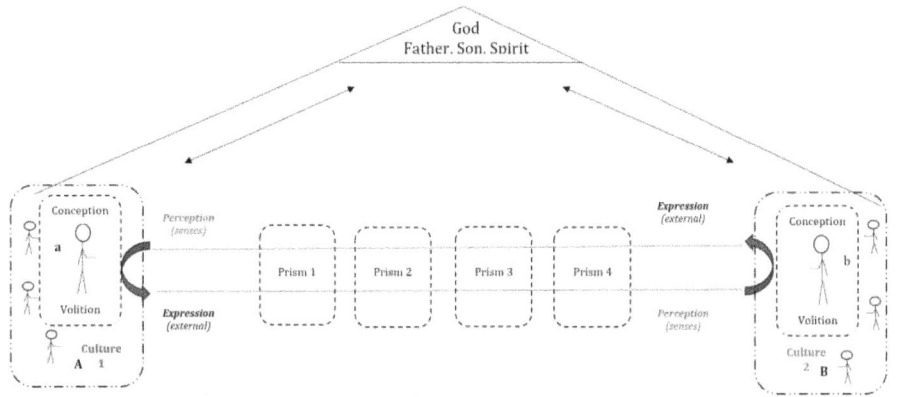

Figure 7. Interactive Model of Relational Communication

The basic outline of RICC is an adaptation and enlargement of previous work by Paul Hiebert.[56] What distinguishes our model from Heibert's model is the recognition that there is always vertical communication to accompany horizontal. Figure 7 demonstrates the idea that communication grows from Father, Son and Spirit as they communicate with One Another and as they communicate vertically with humankind.

Within the vertical and horizontal relationships of Figures 6 and 7 there are four basic processes in the RICC model: perception, conception, volition, and expression. Another point of distinction of RICC from Hiebert's model is the emphasis on "volition" as shown in the figure above.

By **perception** we mean how a person receives and understands a message. Perception is both internal to a given person and external to that person. There is some object that is visible or real: some signal of light or sound waves that really exist. But our human senses do not capture all of the signals that are present. There are several factors which limit what we perceive: our sensory organs may be damaged, so we do not capture all of the signals. We also may have cultural training that makes us aware of one set of signals while ignoring another set of signals. Finally, our personal preferences lead us to perceive some signals that are of particular interest to us and ignore what is not so interesting.

In the RICC model, the senses perceive a signal and then we think about that signal. We are using the word "**conception**" to picture the internal process of thinking or reflecting on something we perceive. This part of the communication process is also internal to us as people: once we perceive a message we begin trying to understand it. Sometimes our thoughts and reflections lead us toward the message as intended by the communicator;

---

[56] Hiebert, *Cultural Anthropology*, 113–137.

sometimes our conception process leads us to misunderstand. Some of the filters that can cause misunderstanding are differences in meaning of words or symbols that were used, so that one person thinks that there was one intention, while the other person meant a different one. Similarly, misunderstandings can take place due to the emotional state of the people involved, or the worldview points of view. Figure 6 lists several factors that affect how we think about what we have perceived.

After conception, the communication process continues with **expression** – the reply or feedback by which one person responds to what another had previously stated. That expression is an external message that is intended to be perceived and understood by the other party in the communication. It is shaped by a mixture of internal and external forces, so that word choice, language used, emotional involvement in communication etc. may affect the expressions that are communicated.

There is one other factor that is central to the RICC model: it is the important element of **volition**. Volition affects every part of the model. We have placed it graphically between conception and expression but in fact, our will is an important part in shaping how we perceive, what we think, and what we express.

Figure 7 shows two other factors that are key to RICC: the prisms and the cultures. Communication is never a straight line between a sender and a receiver. There are many filters that shape what is perceived, what is thought and what is expressed. There could be physical filters (too dark to see, or in the presence of so much noise that hearing was difficult). There could be emotional, volitional prisms (anger, for example, is famous for building misunderstandings). There are also expression issues like the tone of voice, or the language used that can result in difficult communication.

We use the word, "prisms" to talk about these filters between two communicators because prisms have two affects: they divide light into a wider array, allowing some of the rays to go un-perceived. And yet those that are perceived are multiplied in their power. Prisms, you could say, help us to increase the force of a message while also reducing the breadth of that message.

In practical terms, when a message encounters a bad attitude or a language barrier or a concept that runs counter to what was expected the result will be to make the message that is perceived into something different from what was expressed. In the world of intercultural communication, that is a nearly universal experience.

The final part of Figure 7 is the people. There is a person on the left identified as "a." That person comes from a culture A. Between a and A it is likely that a lot of expressive and receptive communication will be understood. Smiles mean the same to both a person and their larger cultural group. Word choices, timetables, and written materials all have similar overlap between the person and that person's cultural group.

But when person "a" speaks to person "b" (from culture B) suddenly we can no longer expect that level of overlap. The meanings of an expression are not apparent. The perceptions are shifted due to a different set of communication patterns and lifetime experiences. What person "b" perceives and conceives (thinks) can easily be quite different from what person "a" had in mind.

The value of RICC is that it allows us to analyze the communication loop that runs from perception to conception to expression. In other words, it allows us to look at the communication process through the lens of what is said, what is understood, what is decided, and what is perceived by the other person.

In the coming pages we will consider this model in more detail, looking especially at the interaction of ideas in a relational, intercultural context.

RICC grows on the foundation of transformational growth

In their volume titled, *Transformational Change in Christian Ministry*, Wan and Raibley build a model of human transformation that develops within the concepts of "being-belonging-becoming.[57]" They present "being" as a reference to the characteristics of an individual. National background, physical attributes, personality traits might all fall into this initial issue in transformational growth.

Their model continues with the idea of "belonging." Horizontal and/or vertical relationships are seen as the environment that fosters transformational growth. From both sociological and theological perspectives, it is the relationship that one has with other people and with the Triune God that shapes us. Belonging, in this respect, is a relational term that points toward interaction.

"Becoming" is the word that Wan and Raibley use to describe the growth and transformation of people. We grow, we change due to the relationships that we are involved with ("becoming" grows from "belonging").

There is much parallel between the RICC model that we are proposing and the being-belonging-becoming view of transformative change.

"Being" is related to the RICC phases of "perception" and "conception." Those two elements of communication (perception and conception) take place largely within a person. They are internal processes that receive communication based largely on such individual issues as previous experiences, previous knowledge, physical and social situation, or mental

---

[57] Wan and Raibley, *Transformational Change in Christian Ministry*.

and physical acuity. The "being" of the receiver shapes what they understand of a given message and how they may respond to that message.

Belonging, in the transformational change model, is closely related to the community of people who are communicating together. The RICC model will speak of three levels of "belonging."

First, there are the people directly involved in a specific communication event. The "sender" and "receiver" may be referred to as a dyad for the sake of simplicity. They come from different backgrounds. Sometimes those backgrounds are closely related (think of two brothers who grew up in the same household). Sometimes the backgrounds are quite different – consider a 60 year-old woman from the United States who is teaching a 25 year old man from Kenya. The obstacles that make "belonging" a challenge between any two people are multiplied when genders, ages, cultural backgrounds, language backgrounds, educational levels, economic and status levels are all distinct.

Second, there are "belonging" issues based on the audiences that surround those primary communicators. The American woman and the younger Kenyan both have other people in their lives: other community members who are part of "belonging." Professional and personal "belonging" both flavor the communication process.

Finally, God is part of all communication. The "belonging" that we see and feel in our horizontal communication is also affected by the presence and activity of Triune God.

Being and belonging are parallel to the RICC model in several ways. We maintain that "becoming" is likewise part of the RICC model. When a person has heard the message and has given it thought (conception), there is a response – an expression. That "expression" will show the way that the message is received. In some cases, expression is part of a process of growth or change (i.e. transformative.)

That change does not necessarily have to be large. There are messages that cause small changes too. The phone call that says, "I can't come to lunch after all" might not change the heart of the recipient, but it will probably change their lunchtime schedule.

Being, belonging and becoming have their relationship with the RICC ideas of perception, conception and expression. There is one other important element of RICC: volition. Across all levels of being-belonging-becoming and across all communication phases of perception-conception-expression, the volition of the parties involved is a leading factor. We commonly hear that "a man hears what he wants to hear." Perception is tied to volition. Similarly, our thinking and expressions are tied to our desires for how to respond to a situation and what future to seek. Volition is active in shaping our being, our belonging within community interaction, and the influences and outcomes that result: our becoming.

RICC grows on the foundation of Relational Interactive Communication

RICC is related to other constructions of interactive communication. Of special interest are the concepts of symmetry, complementarity, reciprocity and schizogenesis. These terms were first used to describe relationships by Bateson, beginning in 1935.[58]

Reciprocity expresses the concept that patterns of behavior or communication will combine or interact with one another. The concept of reciprocity is seen as sequential; taking place across time as one party responds to previous messages. There are two forms of reciprocity: symmetrical and complementary.

Symmetry describes reciprocal relationships that mirror one another. Two athletes in competition, for instance, will each play the same game against the other. There is a relationship, but the exchange is like for like. Other such expressions of symmetrical relationships could include boasting/boasting, opposing/opposing, agreeing/agreeing.[59]

Complementarity refers to reciprocal relationships in which expressions are opposites of one another: "for example, assertion/submission, question/answer, giving/receiving etc."[60]

Reciprocity tends to strengthen relationships. It is used as an illustration of cybernetics, where feedback at the end of one cycle becomes input at the beginning of the next. Cybernetics is the larger trans-disciplinarian study of systems that are self-maintaining and self-correcting. Reciprocal relational communication often has that sort of self-maintaining characteristic.

On the other hand, some relationships create increased differentiation between people. The term, "schismogenesis" was used by Bateson to describe these kinds of relational patterns. Whether fueled by animosity or simply differences in opinion and purpose, relational patterns are not always self-strengthening. It is important to recognize that some patterns move toward division and separation.

One final element of relational interactionism as it is seen in current literature is the fact that patterns are generally predictable, but human beings have an aversion to overly redundant patterns. We like a level of spontaneity and fluidity.[61] This preference for changes and fluidity means that within our relationships, we are likely to change in our posture toward

---

[58] Gregory Bateson, *Steps to an Ecology of Mind*, Ballantine book (New York: Ballantine Books, 1972), 61–72.
[59] Rogers and Escudero, *Relational Communication*, 12.
[60] Rogers and Escudero, *Relational Communication*, 12.
[61] Rogers and Escudero, *Relational Communication*, 18–19.

one another from time to time. Relationship may be complementary (for example), but it will likely show some variations in how that is expressed.

A related perspective on relational interactionism is the need to know what we mean by "relationship" in the first place. Far from being just a shorthand for "friendship," it turns out to be a dynamic and complicated concept. Natalie Kim has identified five elements that help to understand any given relationship[62]:

Beings/beings refers to the nature of the Divine or created beings that are part of the relationship.

Context refers to the variety of places where interaction could take place: for example, consider how relationships differ when the people primarily interact in a home, a workplace, a public shopping area, or a dance studio.

Closeness refers to the emotional attachment that may or may not exist between people. Whether it is "friendliness" or "aloofness" we know that there are differing levels of emotional closeness that exist between people. Sociologist Robin Dunbar[63] has suggested that human beings have a limit for the number of relationships we can handle at any given time. While there is some controversy about the actual number of relationships that a person might be capable of maintaining, yet the foundational truth is certain: as finite human beings we can only be cognizant of and emotionally attuned to a limited number of people. Some of those people will be close to us in terms of emotional involvement, time involvement and willingness to interact. Others will be less "close."

Culture speaks to the norms and patterns that a group considers appropriate between people. Some cultures, for example, greatly restrict the interaction between men and women. Other cultures encourage those same interactions.

Influence describes the outcomes of a relationship; the goal that one or both parties have for the interaction. A teacher, for example, might genuinely like their students but even so the intention of both teacher and student is to see the student graduate and move into the next phase of life. Another relational pair might be pastor and congregant, where the influence sought is growth in living a God-honoring life. An employer/employee pair might seek relationship in order to provide work and strengthen professional skills. There could be genuine good-will between the two, but the influence being sought is nonetheless valid.

---

[62] Enoch Wan and Natalie Kim, *Relational Intercultural Training for Practitioners of Business As Mission: Theory and Practice* (Western Academic Publishers, 2022), 75–94.

[63] R.I.M. Dunbar, "Coevolution of Neocortical Size, Group-Size and Language in Humans," *Behavioral and Brain Sciences* 16 (1992): 681–694.

A Closer Look at Four Phases of Communication in the RICC Model

Figures 6 and 7 guide the introduction of a paradigm of Relational Intercultural Communication (RICC). These figures demonstrate several important factors concerning our model of RICC.

First, Figures 6 and 7 make it clear that our model includes both vertical and horizontal communication.

Secondly, both the vertical and horizontal arrows have arrow heads on both ends, representing a mutual, bi-directional impact.

A third communication issue is that everyone is surrounded by secondary audience members. We are not simply looking at a communication dyad of two people.

Fourth, we can see several variables that may or may not become obstacles to clarity of communication. These variables are social, cultural and personal characteristics that exist between the members of the dyad, and which may be an obstacle to good communication.

Fifth, communication is the process by which we see being-belonging-becoming. It is not a passive "belonging" that we find in human transformation; it is the dynamic interaction between beings/Beings that shape us, change us, help us grow, and in fact bring about transformation.

Figures 6 and 7, together with the text below, guide us deeper into our model of relational intercultural communication.

Communication is a process that includes four interrelated and interactive phases: perception, conception, volition, and expression. Some of these phases occur externally to the people involved, but all four of the phases include at least some internal factors. This mixture of internal/external is part of the reason for the complexity and difficulty in defining exactly what is meant by communication.[64]

Perception

Perception refers to what we sense. It has to do with stimuli that are detected by human sensory organs, and in this regard it is external. It is also, though, internal. We do not perceive all the stimuli that bombards us daily; as finite beings, we have limited and to a degree selective perception.

This becomes important for all communication but is especially important in intercultural communication. Parents of children around the world have had the experience of helping (at times with frustration) them to perceive some stimuli that are especially important for that culture. For example, the color of a street signal (green to go, red to stop), the signs used

---

[64] Griffin, Ledbetter, and Sparks, *A First Look at Communication Theory 10th Edition*, 5.

to indicate restroom facilities for men and the different signs to indicate the ladies' room, or the significance of the number of candles on a birthday cake. These are not at all universal communication devices; they are used in some cultures, not in other cultures. Children who grow up in a culture are taught to respond to some of the stimuli around them, while they may safely disregard other stimuli.

We perceive across a wide range of stimuli, many of which are used deliberately by human cultural groups to communicate. Donald K. Smith discusses twelve "signal systems."[65] Other authors divide intercultural communication into fewer categories: usually categorizing into verbal and non-verbal communication.

For our purposes, there is an advantage in seeing human communication through the lens of multiple stimuli. This helps us to discern with better clarity the stimuli that might be used for communication and to compare the reaction to that stimulus across cultures. We will use Smith's twelve "signal systems" to look at the range of stimuli that can be deliberately used to communicate, and which vary in use across cultures.

What we sense	Examples of communication uses
Spoken words	Speech in any of the approximately 7,000 languages in use today
Written words	Written language with specific grammar, syntax, and preferred forms (some cultures use poetry extensively; others do not. Digital communication via text, direct messaging or electronic transmission is a form of written communication)
Numbers	These can be written or spoken, and they frequently (but not exclusively) refer to the quantity of an item. Like the number of candles on a birthday cake or the relative value of one hundred pennies versus one hundred dollars, it is culturally variable.
Two dimensional pictures	We visibly notice pictures which tell us the contents of canned food, the designation of bathrooms, the maps to navigate a city's bus system etc.
Audio	The non-verbal sounds that we perceive, for example, music, tone of voice, non-verbal utterances. We also have various alarms to wake us up or alert us to danger. These non-verbal sounds vary across cultures.

---

[65] Donald K. Smith, *Creating Understanding*, 2nd ed. ACT Kenya: CUI. Pp 289-318, "The Signals we Use."

What we sense	Examples of communication uses
Artifact – physical, 3-dimensional things	We perceive the items that surround us, and we assign different cultural meanings to them based on contextual information. A small standing desk can be a professor's lectern; in a church it is a pulpit, and in a music hall something very similar holds a musical score.
Kinesic	This is the body language by which people communicate with facial expressions and hand or body gestures. The gestures and expressions are not universal; different cultures assign different meanings to them.
Optical	Humans perceive colors and lights through our eyes. Across cultures, specific colors are given meanings that may be quite different from what other cultures understand.
Tactile	The perception of human touch. When one person touches another, there is a sensory perception of the act; there is also a cultural meaning. Knowing the meaning assigned to being touched requires us to think what kind of touch (a slap compared to a soft tap or a gentle stroke) and also to think what body part is used to touch, and what body part is being touched. A father's touch on his young son's forehead has one meaning; his slap on the son's hand has a different meaning.
Spatial	The perception of distance or space. This can refer to "personal space" for example. It also refers to the typical space preferences for a living space. We can feel crowded; we can also feel separated, isolated.
Temporal	The perception of time. Some things "seem to go fast" while others are "slow, relaxed, leisurely." These distinctions are based on perceptions of the interval between successive events and also culturally conditioned to tell us what is "fast" and what is "slow."
Olfactory	Our senses of smell and taste are powerful parts of human perception and also carry physical and cultural information. Physically we react by rejecting food that smells rotten or tastes as if it has "gone bad." Culturally we teach one generation after another to appreciate some foods and some smells, and to respond with disgust to others.

Figure 8. Perception and Human Senses

Communication factors related to perception

Thinking about how the human body interacts with our environment to sense a stimulus, we can begin to understand some of the factors that are important for communication. These factors become important to analyze for successful intercultural communication. Figure 9 gives details and examples of the communication factors that relate to this level of perception.

Communication factors related to perception	Examples of cultural variations	Examples of potential causes of mis-communication
Physical ability to perceive: acuity of sight, hearing, touch, etc.	Text-based communication poses challenges to people with problems of sight. Music and spoken language can pose problems for those with hearing impairments.	Using print that is too small or in script that is unfamiliar. Use of alarms or tones of voice that are unfamiliar or have contrary meanings (inflection of questions in one culture can mean rebuke or alarm in another culture).
Media	One group may prefer text message; another group communicates with voice recordings or full sentence emails.	Direct messaging abbreviations that can be mis-understood across generations and across cultures. Another example is the use of capitalization in a text message which may or may not be understood as the writer intended.
Language used	-There are power dynamics in the choice of language where several languages are possible. -"Register" refers to the technical level of language: e.g. a medical doctor speaking to colleagues will use a highly technical register; speaking to her patient, that doctor may use a common language register	In bi-lingual situations, people may not hear subtle differences of nuance or vocabulary or register in their second language. In mono-lingual situations, people who do not speak that language may feel excluded.

Communication factors related to perception	Examples of cultural variations	Examples of potential causes of miscommunication
Previous experience	Pleasant experiences with food, visual atmosphere, or sound may encourage repeat connection. This is the power of interior designers who create pleasant mixtures of light, odor, space and objects. And yet, negative experiences (e.g. trauma) can lead to perceptions of threat even in non-threatening situations. Those who suffer from PTSD may respond to "triggers", stimuli related to their trauma, even in the absence of on-going threat.	Failure to recognize a group of people's history is in one sense a failure to recognize how they may perceive a given stimulus. Communicators who understand the historical experiences of their audience will deliberately use communication that relates to positive, favorable responses. Especially in war zones or places where many people suffered traumatic experiences, knowing the history includes knowing the "triggers" that may lead to wrong perceptions.

Figure 9. Perception and Culture

Phase one of RICC, then, is to recognize the issues involved in perception. There are physical stimuli external to the human being that are captured, to one degree or another, by the sensory organs that are part of God's design of our human bodies. Those physical stimuli exist, regardless of how we respond.

Perception is more complicated than simply the external stimulus, though. From one generation to another, we teach ourselves what to "see," that is, what to perceive. Anyone who has worked across cultures has had to learn as an adult what the children of that host culture learn through their parents: how to appropriately notice and respond to a given color, a given taste, or a given sound. It is not just a matter of learning to "interpret" (that is part of cognition); we literally do not notice the stimuli that we have not learned to pay attention to. Perception, for that reason, is at once internal and external to the person engaged in communication.

A simple illustration of this principle comes from the world of music. Recently I was in the audience when the music leader of a small band made a public announcement that she had changed keys without telling the band, and that they had followed her without a problem. The amazing thing is that very few of us in the audience were even aware that the key change had happened. Our senses have not been shaped to perceive the changes that, to the musicians, were obvious. Another illustration comes from a skilled chef who was recently telling me about his use of a particular spice. He had me taste two dishes, one with the spice and one without it. I was unable to tell the difference. I imagine that my senses could be honed to detect that spice, but at this point they are not. My perceptive ability has not been trained for that stimulus.

Perceiving, it turns out, is an important part of expression. In her 2025 publication, *Deep Listening,* [66] author Emily Kasriel reviews how speakers are influenced by the way that they are being listened to. She asserts that people who practice good listening habits (part of perceiving) affect such things as the speaker's self-confidence, the emotional tone of the conversation, what topics a speaker will choose to share, how the speaker understands their own message and how they emotionally connect with their topic and their audience.[67] The quality of listening builds a relational interaction that fosters collaboration.[68] As we continue to look at the cycle of perception/conception/volition/expression we need to keep in mind that these phases are not isolated from one another. The way we listen affects what we perceive and it also affects the expressions that our speaker is making. The emotional tone of the interaction will shift depending on the quality of listening. Interestingly, these benefits from good listening do not require that people share the same perspective on the themes being discussed. A good listener can disagree with the speaker and yet still add a positive, healthy interactive element to the relationship.

The area of perception, like all parts of communication, is more than horizontal. There is also a vertical element by which God is involved in our communication. In what way is Triune God involved in human perception?

God is involved in human perception of both vertical and horizontal communication. Thinking first of horizontal, God opens hearts to pay attention and accept His message given by human agents (Acts 16:14). God also opens understanding so that His message, given by human agents, can be conceptualized correctly (Luke 24:45). God can enter into a human gathering with a variety of languages, and miraculously allow people to perceive their own language (Acts 2:6-8).

God shapes our perceptions in other ways. Philippians 4 is a powerful example. He calls us to deliberately avoid dwelling on anxiety-producing thoughts and events, and instead to recall His presence and His good gifts: to

---

[66] Emily Kasriel, *Deep Listening: Transform your Relationships with Family, Friends and Foes*. New York: HarperCollins, 2025.
[67] Kasriel, p 53.
[68] Kasriel p 56.

learn to perceive our circumstances in light of His promises to the point that we respond with "prayer and supplication with thanksgiving" (Philippians 4:6). In the same passage, God calls us to tune our attention so that we perceive "whatever is true, whatever is noble, whatever is right, whatever is of pure, whatever is lovely, whatever is admirable - if anything is excellent or praiseworthy – think about these things" These are all examples shaping what we perceive according to the values of His Kingdom rather than being conformed to the values and perceptions of this world system (Romans 12:1 – 2).

When we think of vertical communication, we learn to perceive spiritual truth as we grow in maturity in Christ. Matthew 11:15 speaks of a spiritual form of selective perception: those who have ears to hear Jesus' message will hear it. In the context of Matthew 11, that refers to those who heard His explanation of the ministry of John the Baptist in the context of the Old Testament prophets and the ministry of Christ. But that fact of spiritual "selective perception" goes further: Matthew 13 explains why Jesus taught with parables. "This is why I speak to them in parables: Though seeing they do not see; though hearing, they do not hear or understand." (Matthew 13:13). The passage continues with a quote from Isaiah 6, in which the people were described as being dull of hearing and having closed their eyes. We learn to perceive in spiritual terms; seeing, we see more. Rejecting what God has offered, we close our eyes and are unable to see more.

Reading through the Gospels, it is hard to miss the number of times that Jesus taught spiritual truths using the vocabulary of human perception: He is the Light of the world, He is the Bread of Life, He offers living water which flows from our innermost being. These physical truths that we perceive with physical senses become a way to teach and understand spiritual truth. At the core, the issue is whether we perceive what is in our environment. Horizontal communication limits itself to perceptions of the physical world, including the community of people around us. God's Kingdom, in the same way, is perceived by those who have ears to hear. God speaks; He is not silent.[69] But not everyone has ears to hear. Paul makes this point in 1 Corinthians 2 where he distinguishes the spiritual man from the natural man. "This is what we speak, not in words taught us by human wisdom but in words taught by the Spirit, explaining spiritual realities with spirit-taught words. The person without the Spirit does not accept the things that come from the spirit of God but considers them foolishness, and cannot understand them because they are discerned only through the Spirit" (1 Cor. 2:13,14).

---

[69] Schaeffer, *The Complete Works of Francis A Schaeffer: Volume 1: A Christian View of Philosophy and Culture.*, 274–352.

Perception and Being

Much of what we have said about perception is internal, even though it is related to the external. Our recognition and understanding of the world outside of ourselves is not purely objective. In fact, the reason why we have research methods in virtually all disciplines of study is precisely because we are notoriously un-objective. We must teach one another to approximate objective perception.

Outside stimuli exists independently of how we experience or perceive it; and yet a large part of our perception has to do with our individual bodies, our experiences, our spiritual and emotional state, and our culture.

An intercultural model that we introduced previously is useful for intercultural education, leadership and communication. The model of "Being-Belonging-Becoming"[70] allows us to build toward a view of communication that is vertically and horizontally relational.

In the specific phase of communication that we call "perception" we suggest that human perception, both vertical and horizontal, is within the umbrella of "being." Our "being" is not a static being; we change and mature; our horizontal and vertical "eyes" learn to see, and our ears become adept at picking up sounds (both figuratively and literally) that we have not heard before. Paul tells us in 1 Corinthians 13 that we now see in part, but we shall see more accurately as we mature and as God works out His Kingdom plans for this world. We are now the children of God; that is our being. We shall grow more into His image and into deeper insight into His likeness; that is "becoming." Communication begins with the concept of perception which relates our "being."

Summary

In physical terms, we perceive based on previous experiences, cultural emphasis, physical attributes like visual and auditory acuity. We perceive based on context and based on likes and dislikes as a person. The outside world exists, but we experience it based largely on our perceptions.

In spiritual terms, we perceive God's work in our midst and His truths according to our experiences with Him (Taste and see that the Lord is good! Psalm 34:8). We grow in the grace and knowledge of the Lord (2 Peter 3:18); growth implying that we add new understanding onto previous understanding, new levels of trust and obedience onto previous levels of trust and obedience. We learn to see now through a reflection (1 Corinthians 13:12), but later we will see Him as He is (1 John 3:2).

---

[70] Wan, Hedinger, and Raibley, *Transformational Growth*.

In spiritual terms, our "being" now is in a time of "already, not yet." We know that we are children of God; but we are not yet all that we shall be. Our perception of spiritual truth is now valid; our being is immature. Our perceptions of Him and His world will change as we grow and as He works out His Kingdom program, and in that growth our "being" will also grow and develop into what is "not yet."

Conception

Conception refers to our understanding. This is the interior work of taking what we have received through our senses and deciding what it means. This is the work of understanding, and it is at once individual and cultural.

It is this level of conception that makes the intercultural world so interesting. Scores of theories exist that explain the various ways that human cultures conceptualize the world around us. For our purposes, we will divide those hundreds of theories into three large sections: as human beings, we understand the world based on 1) social and relational expectations, 2) emotional expectations, and 3) expectations about appropriate communication patterns.

Social/relational expectations

The literature on social/relational expectations across cultures is vast. Beginning with Edward T. Hall and his pioneering work on cultural patterns seen in proxemics, body language, and time as a cultural element[71] there is a stream of authors and researchers who have described how one culture differs from another culture, especially in how they interact socially. Sociologists like Geert Hofstede, Erin Meyer, Fons Trompenaars, Milton Bennett, Darla Deardorff, Jackson Wu, Tom Steffen and David Livermore have created books, courses, and schools of thought about differing patterns of social interaction which are particularly important for intercultural communication. Figure 10 highlights some of the many theories that help us to identify and adjust to differing social expectations within intercultural communication.

---

[71] Edward T. Hall, *The Silent Language*, [1st ed.]. (Garden City, New York: Doubleday & Company, Inc., 1959), accessed January 31, 2025, https://archive.org/details/silentlanguage00hall. *The Dance of Life,* Anchor Books, 1983.

Name of theory	Notable Author/authors	Description of relational patterns
Individualism and collectivism	Harry Triandis Geert Hofstede	Describes the relationship between a person and their group
Power distance	Geert Hofstede	Describes the relationship between a group of people and their leader
Orality/Textuality	Tom Steffen Walter Ong	Describes how people commonly share ideas and information, whether through oral communication or in writing. Patterns of thinking and communicating vary between these two extremes.
Guilt/Innocence, Honor/Shame and Fear/Power	Roland Müller, Jason Georges, Jackson Wu	The means of a culture to exert social pressure to conform: some cultures formalize laws to which a person is either guilty or not; some cultures reward with honor and punish with social shaming. Other cultures act predominantly from fear of spirit beings which is remedied by the power of magic or shamanism.
Indulgence and restraint	Hofstede-insights.com	The difference between cultural groups in how they view a disciplined/restrained lifestyle compared to a more indulgent, relaxed approach.
Long term orientation	Hofstede-insights.com	The relationship a culture has with its future and its past.

Figure 10. Social Interaction and Communication

These relational variables are only part of the sociology of relationship that can be studied across cultures. How people interact across generations;[72] how people interact with teachers, pastors and other leaders; how people are expected to interact within their gender groups, and across gender groups; and the expected relationship between a culture and expatriates who live in their midst are other examples.

Secular sociologist Janet Beavin Bavelas has picked up on the importance of relational interactions as a major issue in communication.[73] She points out that true communication includes involvement by at least two parties, that they will be mutually involved in the process, and that they will each have some kind of impact or influence on the other. Without those mutual,

---

[72] Sadiri Joy Tira, *From Womb to Tomb: Generational Missiology in the 21st Century and Beyond* (PageMaster Publishing, 2024).

[73] Rogers and Escudero, *Relational Communication*, 9–10.

interactive and influential patterns the exchange cannot rightly be called, "communication." With those things, though, we recognize that concepts are shared within a commonly understood framework; a form of communication.

Emotional Expectations

Communication is more than shared social expectations. It is also shared emotional expectations. How cultures do that, though, is a prominent distinction between cultures. Author Batja Mesquita explains how cultures create emotions in her 2022 volume, *Between Us*.[74] Her insightful book describes how some groups create an emotion together. In those cases, the people will interact in such a way that they laugh or cry or smile or grieve. The descriptions are active verbs that tell what is to be done. The emotion is generated together as a group of people "create" the emotional response to a situation.

There are other cultures that envision emotion as a sort of interior state that may be chosen, controlled, or rejected. That interior state is not conceived of as something that develops from human interactions; it more closely resembles a series of entities that dwell in one's innermost being, and which grow stronger or weaker depending on what the person is "feeding" it. The person who becomes angry has been somehow strengthening that inner "anger." The person who grows tender has been nurturing his/her inner care-giver. The person who shows visible frustration is suffering because of feeding expectations which were not satisfied.

Looking at the descriptions above, there is an obvious difference in the kinds of words found in the "between us" versus the "within me" emotional patterns. The "within me" cultures have a wide range of descriptions of emotional states. We would expect descriptive phrases like, "I feel sad, bitter, frustrated, happy, care-free, resolved, at peace or depressed". These are not verbs necessarily. There are many varieties and variations on any given theme. In comparison, "between us" cultures describe their emotions through verbs like "we laughed" or "we cried."

The differences in how emotion is described follow largely along the lines of cultural trends related to Individualism/Collectivism. Where group identity is more pronounced than individual identity, it is likely that emotional responses will grow within the group. Where the individual is the locus of decision making, it makes sense that emotions would also be individualized and understood to be internal to the person.

---

[74] Batja Mesquita, *Between Us: How Cultures Create Emotions* (New York, NY: W. W. Norton & Company, 2022).

The question before us is how people make sense of the circumstances surrounding them. We conceptualize based on cultural patterns of thinking. We also conceptualize based on emotional patterns. In social interaction, we often conceive of a situation based on the emotional response that we have in the moment. This has two strong implications for us.

First, communication is rarely a simple transfer of cognitive information. Whatever the cognitive elements may be, there is always some level of emotional communication at the same time. Knowing that cultures vary in their emotional responses as much as they vary in other cultural patterns should give us pause to consider carefully how we should communicate any given theme. Whether pastoral or educational or regular daily life like shopping and working, it is wise to learn the emotional patterns of a group of people and interact with them appropriately.

As I write this, I (Mark) recall a moment in my multicultural church where we faced a particularly sad time. I come from an "emotions are inside me" culture but the people I was caring for were in the "emotions are between us" culture. I did not know how to grieve with those who grieve, and the result was a feeling on all sides that we did not "connect" at a point where connection was both appropriate and necessary. Of course we learn, sometimes exactly from those difficult moments, but it would have been much better to know how that congregation grieved beforehand, so that in the moment of need the right emotional response could have been displayed.

Second, it is also important to not draw these distinctions between "inside me" and "between us" too firmly. It may be that one group creates emotions "between us" in face-to-face ethos while another culture creates that "between us" feeling through mass media. Consider the film industry; there is a lot of emotion that is shared by those who watch a film; it is part of the planned response that the film industry creates. That is a sort of "between us" emotion (although obviously distinct from the face-to-face emotions that Mesquita describes). Similarly, the ad industry puts great emphasis on developing emotional appeal even as they share cognitive information.

The point is that emotional content differs across cultures, but it is always a part of communication. In some cases, it is generated by interaction within a group. In other cases, the emotion is seen as somehow an inner quality that can be developed or controlled, as a person desires.

Expectations about Communication Patterns

Looking at the exchange of information between members of a culture, we also recognize that communication patterns themselves are part of a culture. One culture prefers face-to-face; another is content with digital communication technology. One culture prefers writing; another prefers oral communication. It is important to note the variety of communication theories which help us to see a panorama of ways that people share with one another. Figure 11 provides a number of examples.

Communication Style	Notable Authors	Description
Particular or universal	Trompenaars	Describes how a group presents information: from the individual case to the generalized concept, or the opposite.
Narrative or propositional	Ong Steffen	Closely related to oral/literate cultures, this focuses on the form of communication; across a continuum from "narrative" story-form to propositional.
Direct/indirect	Hall	Describes the speech patterns within a community; some cultures clearly express any disagreement, doubt, or disapproval that they feel. Those cultures favor "direct" communication. Other cultures express differences in the softest of language, and preferably by way of an intermediary.
High context/low context	Hall	Describes the weight that words carry in comparison with what is assumed from the context; some cultures use the context to carry most meaning; others prefer that words be used to explicitly carry the weight of meaning.
Languages of Culture	Smith	Based on the twelve "signal systems" by which people communicate, the Languages of Culture recognizes that any given cultural group will have its own verbal and non-verbal symbols. To communicate across cultures, knowledge of the language is helpful, but just as important is the knowledge of how all twelve of the languages of culture are used.

Figure 11. Communication Patterns across Cultures

Conception and Vertical Communication

The Kingdom of God has certain patterns that it follows, and citizens of the Kingdom are to teach these patterns to one another. In that way, we can say that the Kingdom of God has its own culture.

It is not a culture based on food and drink (Romans 14:17-20). Nor is it a matter of one language in favor of another (Acts 2:1-13). The Kingdom of

God is not based on a cultural pattern of physical birth, but by the will of God (John 1:13).

The patterns of life that are common to the culture of God's Kingdom have to do with relationships with God and relationships with other people. The patterns that are part of the Kingdom include loving the Lord with all of one's heart and soul and mind and strength, and loving one's neighbor as oneself (Mark 12:30-31). The patterns of the Kingdom have to do with faith (Hebrews 11:6). The patterns of the Kingdom have to do with knowing God and Jesus Christ whom He sent (John 17:3). The patterns of the Kingdom have to do with growing in Christian faith and in a relationship with God (2 Peter 3:18).

One might read this list of characteristics of the Kingdom of God and object that we did not include Bible Knowledge. That is indeed an important element, and it is closely related to this conception phase of communication. There is one sense in which Bible Knowledge is essential for vertical communication. There is also another way in which Bible Knowledge is often misunderstood and in fact is not an element of vertical communication.

In positive terms, knowing the Bible is essential if one is going to live according to the patterns of the Kingdom of God. One cannot have faith without knowing who God is and how He interacts with His people. One needs to know the instructions of the Bible if one is going to follow them. One cannot love God if one does not have any knowledge of who He is or what He does. Clearly knowledge is an important part of being able to conceptualize the Kingdom of God (John 20:31, Romans 12:1-2).

And yet knowledge of facts and figures without knowledge of the Person of God is a stumbling block. The Pharisees of Jesus' day "knew" the Old Testament Scriptures but had no relationship with the God of the Bible (John 5:39). Jesus warns people that performing religious activities is not the same thing as knowing God. In Matthew 7:21-23 He warns us that being active in spiritual terms is not the same as knowing and being known by the Lord; "I never knew you. Away from me, you evildoers" (Matthew 7:21-23) is the sad response to those who know about Christ but do not know Him.

Conceptualizing the Kingdom of God, then, includes study (2 Timothy 2:15) but it does not mistake head knowledge for a personal relationship with Triune God. "In Him we live and move and have our being" (Acts 17:28). That living and moving and being calls for knowledge that goes beyond intellectual assent. It is knowing and relationally interacting with the Persons of Father, Son and Spirit.

Conception and Belonging

Vertical and horizontal levels of intercultural communication are shaped by relational interaction. Horizontal communication takes the shape preferred by the culture of the group, for example by noting and adapting to cultural relational patterns of leadership, gender, and social status. "I have become all things to all people" said Paul in 1 Corinthians 9:19-23. He would adjust to the diet, the relationship patterns, the communication patterns, and the emotional patterns of his audiences.

This level of belonging, though, has limits. Acts 15 relates the story of how the apostles and elders in Jerusalem heard the question of early Gentile believers. Their decision, related by Paul and Barnabas, was that new believers could maintain their previous lifestyle except to "abstain from food polluted by idols, from sexual immorality, from the meat of strangled animals and from blood" (Acts 15:20). Staying clear of idolatry, false gods, and immoral behavior was named as central to conceptualizing relationships across cultures. What we now call "contextualization" is the process of finding those elements of cultures that would drive new believers away from worship of Triune God. But beyond those elements, a vertical relationship can take on many or even most of the patterns of life of the culture in which it is found. RICC points to conception of God's Word and God's Kingdom in such a way as to grow in the grace and the knowledge of the Lord Jesus Christ (2 Peter 3:18). That becomes a relational pattern of Christian life that fits largely within the horizontal patterns of the people, while following vertical patterns in case of discrepancy between horizontal and vertical patterns. In the analysis of Peter's visit with Cornelius, we referred to this as the "inclusion principle" (see figure 3).

Horizontal relationships across cultures likewise are relational. The practitioner of RICC will adapt to the lifestyle of his host culture, will understand the differences compared to his/her own home culture, and will adapt as necessary to build healthy relationships within the new host culture. Knowing how cultural patterns, emotional patterns, and communication patterns operate in the new culture gives one the ability to live and move and be within that culture too – not under the human "law" but under the Law of Christ (1 Cor 9:21).

The being-belonging-becoming motif embraces cultural conception as a part of the "belonging" phase. As we grow in our conceptual understanding of a culture's patterns of life, we find ourselves belonging more and more within that group.

Volition

Some years back I had a conversation with the son of a missionary to West Africa. He was telling me about his father, and how powerfully God had used the father to communicate God's Word to a previously unreached group. The son told me that his father had a significant lack of linguistic ability, telling me that he never did speak the language very well. "How did he communicate the Gospel?" I asked. The answer was that this man so wanted people to know Jesus Christ that he entered into everyday life in a way that no other outsider had ever done. "He ate off of our plates" was the phrase that the son said was repeated to him over and over about his father. The man didn't separate himself into a different lifestyle, but instead he ate and slept and drank and lived with the people. The message became clear because the messenger entered life with the community.

We could look at our previous communication phases and say that this missionary took on the cultural norms of the community so much that his message was understandable even without a strong use of spoken language. We could look at the signal systems and say that this man learned to communicate well with food, objects, and physical proximity even though he did not use the signal system of spoken language.

Yet there is a fundamental question at the root of those efforts: Why? What motivated him to give of himself to that level? What motivated him to admit that his language was weak but that he could still learn other ways to make Christ known? What was the power that kept him from discouragement and that, to the contrary, led him to second and third efforts at communicating?

The issue of will, of volition, is in view here. For the most part, this is a topic that is ignored by the standard texts in communication. For the most part, this is a topic that is replaced by discussion about technique and methodology. But the authors of this book maintain that volition, the will to decide and persevere in that decision, is key to RICC.

Let us consider an example of horizontal communication. One person expresses an idea, a thought. The other perceives that stimulus and hears the voice or sees the text message or picks up the note left on his desk. There is expression. There is perception.

The message can then be conceptualized – some level of understanding is determined about the meaning of that message. Now comes the moment of volition. How does the recipient of that message decide to respond?

Suppose that the message is a short, written note left on a desk that simply says, "Let's go out for lunch today."

If the author of the note and the recipient are good friends who occasionally go out for lunch, then the "will" to say yes will likely only be hampered if some other responsibility is in the way. "Yes! I'd love to" would be an easy answer. Likewise, "I would love to, but I have a report that needs to be done, and I have to work over lunch to get it finished" is likewise an easy answer. The will is there in either case.

But what if the context is different and the writer of that short note has had a long-standing disagreement with the invitee? What if there are personal frictions involved that have strained relationships over the years? What if in the recipient of the note there is a feeling of dread. "I don't want to go out to lunch with that guy. He never has anything good to say. He will just criticize me again on the same old topic."

The same short note in a more problematic context leads to a very distinct response. At the heart of that second response is volition. "I don't want to."

The Bible and the Will

The Bible speaks frequently and powerfully about the place of volition in communication between God and people. For example, Colossians 1:27, "God willed to make known what is the riches of the glory of this mystery among the Gentiles, which is Christ in you, the hope of glory."[75] This act of communication by Triune God to humankind is attributed to God's will.

From the human side, we perceive God's voice and understand His message as a result of our will. In John 7:17 Jesus says, "Anyone who chooses to do the will of God will find out whether my teaching comes from God or whether I speak on my own."

There are two primary word groups in New Testament Greek that give the sense of volition, will, wish, or take pleasure in.[76] Between those word groups, there are over 130 uses in the New Testament. Beyond the lexical information, the concept of God's good will or His pleasure is a concept that is repeated frequently in Scripture. For example, Paul's prayer in Ephesians 3:14ff is of special importance. Paul prays to God that His people "might be able to comprehend with all the saints what is the breath and length and height and depth and to know the love of Christ which surpasses knowledge.[77]" Paul's prayer was that God would be willing and active to open human perception and understanding. Vertical communication is a key to relational intercultural communication; without God's gracious involvement we only share concepts. With His gracious involvement, vertical

---

[75] The New American Standard Bible (NASB) translation shows the idea of "will" strongly in this verse. The NIV captures the idea with its rendering, "God has chosen... "

[76] Brown, *The New International Dictionary of New Testament Theology*, 3:1015–1026.

[77] NASB translation

communication can flower into a depth of comprehension that goes beyond our ability to understand.

Besides the importance of divine and human will in vertical communication, the volitional phase of communication is also important in horizontal communication.

It can be important in simply human-to-human terms. A wise teacher or leader or communicator knows that if the will of the audience is engaged, it is much easier to lead toward the goals that are in mind. Similarly, if the will is not engaged then it is next to impossible to see progress in that educational, leadership, or communicatory relationship. As the adage goes, "a man convinced against his will remains unconvinced still."

Figure 12 shows at least three ways that horizontal communication can be shaped according to the volitional states of the people involved.

Volitional outcome	Example from Scripture	Communication principle
Godly decisions	"I urge you…in view of God's mercy to offer your bodies as a living sacrifice" Romans 12:1	Engaging the will as part of communicating the importance of godly decisions and lifestyle
Godly relationships	"Come to Me all you who are weak and burdened" Matthew 11:28-29	Engaging the will is part of an invitation to relationship with Christ
God honoring ministry	"Eagerly desire the greater gifts" 1 Corinthians 12:30-13:13	Engaging the will is part of developing ministry gifts.

Figure 12. Communication and Volition

As important as the will is in setting a positive, transformational trajectory for life and ministry, it is just as involved in creating a negative, transgressional lifestyle. Isaiah 14:13-14 lists five "I wills" spoken by Satan in his rebellion. Those expressions of volition show how self-will stands in contrast to a will that seeks to know and to serve God:

> You said in your heart, I will ascend to the heavens;
> I will raise my throne above the stars of God,
> I will sit enthroned on the mount of assembly,
> On the utmost heights of Mount Zaphon.
> I will ascend above the tops of the clouds;
> I will make myself like the Most High."

The reason for biblical warnings against grumbling and complaining comes into focus in light of the important role that volition plays in communication. "Do not let any unwholesome talk come out of your mouths, but only what is helpful for building others up according to their needs" (Eph. 4:29) is tied directly to human willingness. We have all experienced the way a bad attitude can spread and negatively affect a group of people. One of the core mechanisms in that contagious process is the will of the people involved. Negative talk undermines the will to grow and change in positive relational elements like faith, hope and love. Negative talk instead supports the transgressional process toward rejecting God and godly influences.

One of the most profound examples of the effects of unwholesome communication is found in Exodus 16. God had met every need of the people of Israel in their journey out of bondage and into the freedom of the Promised Land. God was leading them and providing daily for every need. God provided human leadership through Moses and Aaron, and made it clear that they were leading at God's direction.

Even with this extensive Divine involvement, in Exodus 16:2 and following we read that the people "grumbled against Moses and Aaron" over the issue of food. In Exodus 17:3, the grumbling arose again about the issue of water to drink. From desiring physical water, the complaints shifted to verbal attacks on Moses and Aaron. In 17:3 rather than asking for water, the people accused Moses of bringing the people up from Egypt "to make us and our children and livestock die of thirst." The complaining led Moses to even fear for his life: he asked, "What am I to do with these people? They are almost ready to stone me" (Ex. 17:4).

The negative communication, growing from a will directed to complaint rather than trust, led to increasing conflict between Moses and the people. Open idolatry grew as Aaron fashioned the golden calf seen in Exodus 32.

Human, horizontal communication and human volition are tightly connected. As we encourage one another to love and good works (Heb 10:24), we are communicating toward positive, godly transformative ends. But communication that is negative, even if it begins as relatively small and mild, can lead to transgression and rejection of God's ways.

Application of volition in RICC

There are several important points of application regarding volition in RICC:

1. Some communication difficulties may be a problem of volition. There are times when intercultural communication breaks down because of erroneous perceptions or cultural patterns that are not understood, it is true. But there are other instances when failure in

communication grows from volitional problems. The response is to engage the will as part of a communication process.
2. It is also important to listen carefully for the direction of expressed will. Those whose volition is aimed at serving God and people can be equipped with cultural understanding and communication skills. But a willful desire to serve self will lead astray even if cultural understanding is high.

Summary

When we think of intercultural communication, volition takes an important role of motivation and direction for perception, for expression, and for cognition. Relational interactionism describes communication as dynamic. The direction of that dynamism is influenced by volition.

The will to love the Lord our God is at the heart of vertical communication, and the will to love our neighbor as ourselves is at the core of horizontal communication. For that reason, Paul spends so much time in 1 Corinthians 13 to explain "a better way" of communicating to replace the noisy gong and clanging cymbal of communication that lacks the will to love.

Expression

The cycle of RICC goes from the external/internal dynamism of perception to the internal world of comprehension where it is shaped by volitional forces. After that, the cycle moves back outside of the person through the external expression of thoughts, feelings, emotions to which another person or Person may interact.

The four processes that we have focused on (perception, conception, volition and expression) form a cycle. In this RICC book, we have presented them as if they form an ordered series, but that is only for the sake of presentation. In reality the cycle can begin with expression, which another person may perceive, conceptualize and decide to act upon. Or the cycle might start within the internal thoughts of a person's mental conception, later taking shape through volition, expression and resulting perception by another person. The point is that this is a cycle without a fixed entry point or exit point. Relational intercultural communication, being cyclical in nature, is able to begin and end at multiple places along the model.

In the cycle of communication as we have presented in this book, we now find an expression in response to what has been perceived, understood, and volitionally decided. This is an external process that is based on the internal understanding of the previous three steps (perception, conception, volition).

The phase of communication that we are calling "expression" will be shaped by factors that we have already seen as important in communication. Figure 13 highlights important factors that affect the communicative decisions we make in expressing ourselves.

Factor affecting Expression	Definition/Description	Example
Signal system	Deliberate expression of specific verbal and non-verbal communications to form a message.	Touching a grieving person's hand while giving words of condolence. In other cultures, not touching a grieving person while giving condolences. In other cases, the touch may carry meaning without words.
Register of language	The vocabulary choices used for expression	For a professional group, use of technical language. For a lay group, more daily-use language. For children, expression through simple illustration
Interpersonal relationship	The appropriate level of expression depending on gender, family relationship, ages involved, etc.	One who learns to communicate within a culture will learn what to share within the "in-group" and what to share with "outsiders." Similarly, what to share with different groups even within the larger culture (e.g. men/women, old/young).
Previous experience	Sensitivity to the hearer's previous experiences as a guide to expression	Avoiding trigger words for those who have gone through traumatic circumstances.
Media use	Choices among media options such as oral, written, digital, presential, recorded etc.	Adjusting to the media preferences of the audience so that expressions can be received with minimal confusion.
Social hierarchy	Expression will be shaped by the relative social levels of those involved	A worker in a company in some cultures may only state polite, positive things to the manager, yet in other cultures workers freely express even negative opinions.

Figure 13. Factors that Influence Expression

In the RICC model, expression is the phase of communication which flows from the perception of a message, the conception of what that message means, and the volitional decision about how to respond. Expression in horizontal terms will be shaped by many of the elements that have been seen in the previous phases of communication (signal systems, context, previous experience etc.).

RICC expression and the expat

There is no single answer to the question of how an expat should express himself in communication with members of a host culture. The expat should learn and grow in awareness of the differences between expressive norms of their home culture and expressive norms of the host culture. The expat should likewise be careful to learn and avoid expressions which are insulting or demeaning in the host culture. Finding ways to express oneself that are considered well-mannered and culturally appropriate will help take the focus off the speaker and instead allow the message to be in view. Deliberate effort is needed for an expat to learn the pathways of verbal and non-verbal communication that are common, appropriate, and understood in a host culture, and then as an expat to adapt to meet those pathways.

Returning to Figure 7, there are a series of obstacles to perception and expression that are graphically shown toward the bottom of the figure, called "prisms" in the figure. Those represent barriers to communication. Of course, we know that within a given culture there are many barriers and obstacles that create misunderstandings and confusion. But those barriers and obstacles are multiplied many times over in cross cultural communication. The filters that are found across the bottom section of Figure 7 give us a starting point at what things the expat needs to deliberately learn in order to communicate well within a host culture.

RICC and vertical expression

Expression is part of vertical communication. The worship that we bring to our relationship with Triune God, and the prayers that we offer are two examples of expressive communication brought into a vertical relationship.

Psalm 19 is an expression of David's heart toward God; he creates a parallel between God's vertical communication toward humankind as seen in creation and as seen in God's Word. David shapes his reply to express his adoration for the works and Word of God, recognizing God's Word for its power in restoring the soul, making wise the simple, bringing joy to the heart and so on. David is responding to God, but in that response, we see an expression of wonder, of appreciation, of gratitude. At the end of the Psalm,

David prays that the words expressed by his mouth and the intentions found in the meditation of his heart would be acceptable to Almighty God.

In a similar way, Paul exhorts the Thessalonian church to rejoice, to pray without ceasing, to give thanks, and to respond positively to prophetic utterances. Those commands are related to human expression toward God.

The Bible also teaches that human horizontal expressions have an impact on our vertical relationship. Matthew 5:22 warns that the mis-use of horizontal communication can bring about vertical condemnation. The answer, in verses 23-24, is to reconcile with people (which requires communication) in order to maintain a good relationship with God.

Expression, RICC, and Becoming

RICC is our tool for looking at interactive communication across cultures. In previous phases of the communication process, we have seen how

> Perception deals with Being.
> Conception deals with Belonging
> Volition is a personal response of relative willingness to be, belong and become.

We maintain that expression is, at times, aimed at "becoming." The expression of one's thoughts, emotions, dreams, and will can be done with the desire to shape exterior reality to fit the internal wishes, understanding and feelings of the speaker. Expression is related to "becoming."

We also readily admit that most people do not consciously see their communication in that way. Rarely if ever do we deliberately think, "I want to change the reality outside of myself by the use of my words and expressions." But in essence, that is what happens when we express ourselves. We are presenting our understanding of reality and our wishes for the future with a level of hope that our words will reflect reality and influence others' understanding and motivations within that reality.

God encourages us to consider our language as related to reality: if we confess with our mouth that Jesus is Lord and believe that God raised Him from the dead we will be saved (Rom. 10:9). It is both an interior belief and an exterior expression. In fact, Paul continues in Romans 10 with the clarification that "for it is with your heart that you believe and are justified, and it is with your mouth that you profess your faith and are saved" (Rom. 10:10).

Similarly, the expression of God's Word is "sharper than any double-edged sword" (Heb. 4:12). The Lord says that His Word "will not return to Me empty, but will accomplish what I desire" (Isa. 55:11). The Word of God is "a lamp for our feet," meant to guide our decisions (Ps. 119:105).

All of these biblical passages point to a power of expression that goes well beyond our typical view. In fact, Jesus warns us that the expression of our words is of eternal significance. Speaking to the Pharisees, He said,

> You brood of vipers, how can you who are evil say anything good? For the mouth speaks what the heart is full of. A good man brings good things out of the good stored up in him, and an evil man brings evil things out of the evil stored up in him. But I tell you that everyone will have to give account on the day of judgment for every empty word they have spoken. For by your words you will be acquitted, and by your words you will be condemned." (Matt. 12: 34-37).

Summary

This chapter focuses on presenting a model of RICC. That model is based on four phases of communication which together align with relational concepts of being, belonging and becoming. Figure 14 summarizes how these phases of communication interact with relational interactionist theory.

Communication Phase	Description of alignment in horizontal communication	Relational Interactionist Theory
Perception	Human communication perception is the internal and external process by which external stimuli are received. A person's sensory acuity, previous experiences and cultural conditioning strongly affect perceptions of the stimuli around us.	being
Conception	Conception is the internal process of understanding what was perceived. It is heavily shaped by cultural patterns of normal, acceptable use of signal systems and the relational interactions within a culture.	belonging
Volition	Human communication is shaped by the will of the people involved.	Perception: we see what we want to see. Conception: we understand what we wish to understand. Expression: we communicate according to our will.
Expression	Human communication may seek to reflect and shape reality by the expressions a communicator uses. We use words and other communication acts to create in others the perspective that we have of reality and future. It is the expression of our view and our will.	becoming

Figure 14. Four Phases of Relational Interactive Communication

Within this being-belonging-becoming motif, we return to the idea of relational interactionism. As phrased by Enoch Wan, reality is relationship, first vertical and then horizontal.[78] This view of reality is strongly supported

---

[78] Enoch Wan, "The Paradigm of 'Relational Realism,'" *Occasional Bulletin* 19, no. 2 (2006): 1–4.

by our investigation into RICC. Relationships lead us to know what and how to perceive, to conceive, to will, and to express.

Conclusion

This chapter has built a theory of Relational Intercultural Communication (RICC). The starting point for the chapter was a review of contemporary theories about communication. Following that, communication was seen in light of transformational growth and relational interactionism. Those topics then became the foundation for a detailed review of communication that is at once vertical and horizontal, and that also exists in the four phases of perception, conception, volition and expression.

CHAPTER 5
INTERCULTURAL RELATIONAL QUOTIENT (IRQ): TOWARDS GREATER INTERCULTURALITY IN INTERCULTURAL INTERACTIONS AND COMMUNICATION

Hannah Kappler and Enoch Wan

Introduction

Intercultural communication involves more than the exchange of information or translation of a message between two languages. It is a complex process of relational transformation, where interactions between two or more cultures offer potential for mutual growth and understanding. This chapter will introduce Intercultural Relational Quotient (IRQ), discuss its philosophical foundations, contrast IRQ to other popular approaches to intercultural interaction, unpack the theoretical underpinnings of IRQ within Wan's relational interactionism[79], consider the role of IRQ in intercultural communication, examine the practical application of IRQ in different intercultural communication, and provide a framework for understanding how cultivating a high IRQ leads to greater interculturality in our increasingly interconnected world. This chapter posits that IRQ, a measure of an individual's capacity to cultivate deep, influential relationships across cultures, serves as a catalyst for achieving genuine interculturality within the relational interactionism framework.

Intercultural Relational Quotient: Definition, Purpose, and Motivations

Intercultural Relational Quotient (IRQ) is defined as a measure of an individual's ability to nurture and maintain depth and influence in interactions with others in a cultural context outside of the one(s) to which the individual belongs. This definition highlights several key aspects of relationships, framed within an intercultural context. The multidimensional capacity to cultivate deep, influential relationships across cultural boundaries hinges on five core aspects, synthesized by Kim from Robert Hinde's components of relationships and Enoch Wan's relational epistemology: Beings/beings, interaction, context, depth, and influence.[80] Understanding IRQ through the lens of these five core aspects reveals its

---

[79] Enoch Wan – references on relational interactionism in Appendix 1.
[80] Wan and Kim, *Relational Intercultural Training for Practitioners of Business As Mission: Theory and Practice*, 115.

potential, moving beyond the mere acquisition of cultural knowledge to the development of transformative intercultural relationships.

Beings/beings: IRQ encompasses not only interactions between human beings but, within the relational interactionism framework, also extends to relationships with and among angelic beings and the Beings of the Trinity. The Trinity in its very essence models perfect relationality between the Father, Son, and Holy Spirit (John 17:21). This divine interplay of relationships serves as the archetype for human relationships, inspiring us to move beyond transactional interactions towards a model of love, service, and mutual edification.

Interaction: IRQ emphasizes the dynamic nature of intercultural engagement. It recognizes that communication across cultures is a complex dance and a constant negotiation of meaning and understanding which requires active listening, empathy, and adaptability. Intercultural exchanges inherently require interaction between two or more distinct and culturally unique parties. This element of interaction acknowledges the unscripted nature of intercultural exchanges which involve two or more beings.

Context: Context is critical to relationships, and all intercultural interactions occur within a specific context. Cultural norms, values, and communication styles vary significantly in cultures, necessitating cultural sensitivity and the ability to adapt one's communication style to align with the specific cultural context.

Depth: IRQ prioritizes depth of relationship over superficiality, emphasizing the importance of cultivating meaningful connections with individuals from other cultures. This requires genuine curiosity, trust, empathy, and a willingness to move beyond stereotypes and preconceived notions to achieve true understanding. While not directly correlated to depth, the longevity of a relationship may be a supplemental marker of depth.

Influence: IRQ empowers individuals to exert positive influence in intercultural settings, not through imposition but through fostering collaboration, building consensus, and working together to achieve shared goals. This necessitates effective communication, conflict resolution skills, and the ability to build bridges of understanding across cultural divides.

IRQ and relational intercultural communication emphasize the importance of building meaningful connections and fostering genuine understanding between individuals from different cultural backgrounds. Communication is not merely about transmitting information but also about creating shared meaning, building trust, and navigating cultural differences with sensitivity and respect. Rather than simply falling under the umbrella of intercultural competence, IRQ takes an alternative approach by prioritizing the building of relationships. IRQ does not ignore or overlook the valuable advances and research within the field of intercultural competency; rather, it recognizes the strengths of intercultural competence models while seeking to highlight a relational perspective to intercultural interactions and communication.

Current Approaches to Intercultural Interactions

Intercultural competence (IC) is the prevailing approach to analyzing intercultural interactions, from which intercultural communicative competence also stems. Imahori and Lanigan observed that existing models of intercultural competence tend to emphasize one or two out of the following components: behavior (skill), motivation (attitude), or knowledge (cognition).[81] These three categorizations form the basis of a wide variety of models which are used to understand intercultural competence. Literature has expressed the need for more integrated or holistic approaches which not only combine these elements of cognitive awareness, character traits, and social skills but also integrate a more intercultural perspective into the concept itself.[82]

Intercultural competence encompasses a broad spectrum of concepts while also serving as a general term for one aspect of intercultural abilities.[83] The extensive range of material available and models associated with intercultural competence can largely be attributed to the absence of a unified definition for the term. Varied interpretations regarding its fundamental nature and suitable application result in differing perspectives on its component competences and whether it is something that can be acquired.[84]

Scholars such as Hofstede, Trompenaars and Hampden-Turner, and Livermore have provided substantial contributions to the field; however, the predominance of Western perspectives risks imposing a culturally biased view of competence. The current Eurocentric approach can inadvertently discount non-Western ways of knowing and interacting, which may be

---

[81] T. Todd Imahori and Mary L. Lanigan, "Relational Model of Intercultural Communication Competence," *Special Issue: Intercultural Communication Competence* 13, no. 3 (January 1, 1989): 270–272.

[82] T. Todd Imahori et al., "Intercultural Communication Competence: Identifying Key Components from Multicultural Perspectives," *International Journal of Intercultural Relations* 29, no. 2 (March 2005): 137. "Probing Intercultural Competence in Malaysia: A Relational Framework," ed. B. Mohamad and H. Abu Bakar, *SHS Web of Conferences* 33 (2017): 1, https://doi.org/10.1051/shsconf/20173300045.

[83] Kwok Leung, Soon Ang, and Mei Ling Tan, "Intercultural Competence," *Annual Review of Organizational Psychology and Organizational Behavior* (2014): 490.

[84] Stefanie Rathje, "Intercultural Competence: The Status and Future of a Controversial Concept," *Language and Intercultural Communication* 7, no. 4 (April 4, 2007): 255, accessed March 25, 2024, https://papers.ssrn.com/abstract=1533596.

equally valid and effective in their own cultural contexts. This imbalance reinforces a narrative where Western standards are seen as the norm, thus marginalizing other cultural paradigms.

Intercultural competence denotes the ability to function effectively and appropriately in diverse cultural contexts, and it often encompasses a wide range of skills, including cultural awareness, adaptability, empathy, and the ability to manage uncertainty and ambiguity. The emphasis of intercultural competence is placed on achieving successful adaptation and minimizing misunderstandings in intercultural interactions. "Intercultural competence, in spite of its importance, is perhaps too often considered a 'magic bullet' that provides a guarantee for success in situations that are very complex and also 'happen' to be intercultural."[85] As a result, intercultural competence can be considered as an elusive and mystical skill which gives people extraordinary ability to navigate situations which would be challenging even in monocultural contexts.

Intercultural Communicative Competence

Intercultural communication has been a field of study for approximately 50 years, with Hall often credited as its founding figure.[86] One key area of focus for researchers has been the exploration of intercultural communicative competence (ICC). This framework narrows the focus to the specific communication skills required for successful communicating a message across cultures, emphasizing linguistic proficiency, nonverbal sensitivity, message decoding, and the ability to adapt communication styles to different cultural contexts. The goal is to achieve effective and appropriate communication that leads to desired outcomes.

ICC holds significance for both academics and practitioners involved in intercultural interactions within diverse settings such as training programs, living abroad, and navigating daily multicultural encounters. Defining ICC proves challenging due to the subjective nature of competence and its reliance on cultural contexts. Despite advancements since Hall's contributions, a comprehensive model of ICC and a universally applicable scale are yet to be developed.[87]

While building upon the broader notion of intercultural competence, ICC often falls into the same trap of privileging Western perspectives. While numerous models of ICC exist, they often emphasize elements like linguistic

---

[85] Hoffman and Verdooren, *Diversity Competence*, 62.
[86] Lily A. Arasaratnam and Marya L. Doerfel, "Intercultural Communication Competence: Identifying Key Components from Multicultural Perspectives," *International Journal of Intercultural Relations* 29, no. 2 (March 2005): 138.
[87] Arasaratnam and Doerfel, "Intercultural Communication Competence," 138.

fluency, direct communication styles, and assertive self-expression, reflecting values prevalent in many Western cultures. However, these values are not universally shared. For example, prioritizing verbal fluency may inadvertently undervalue communication styles prevalent in high-context cultures, where meaning is often conveyed subtly through nonverbal cues and contextual understanding. Similarly, valuing direct communication might lead to misinterpretations and discomfort in cultures where indirectness and diplomacy are highly regarded. This Western-centric bias within ICC frameworks risks misrepresenting effective communication as synonymous with Western communication norms, potentially leading to misunderstandings and perpetuating cultural hierarchies in intercultural interactions.

Evangelical Contributions to Intercultural Competence

Evangelical scholars have been involved in the development of intercultural communication theory since the 1950s. Notable figures include linguist Eugene Nida, textbook author and conference organizer John Condon, and founder of Stanford University's Summer Institute of Intercultural Communication, Clifford Clarke. However, as the field has progressed, secular scholars have overlooked the contributions of evangelicals. More recently, well-known evangelical scholars in areas related to IC include communication scholars Charles Kraft and David Hesselgrave, as well as anthropologists Marvin Mayers, Sherwood Lingenfelter, and Paul Hiebert.[88] Moreau, Campbell, and Greener developed an interactionist model of intercultural competence, which recognizes the importance of the integration of cognitive awareness, character traits, and social skills.[89] Evangelicals possess a distinct advantage over their secular counterparts, as they draw not only on the same empirical information available to any anthropologist, but also on insights derived from divine revelation, such as the belief that humans are created in the image of God, imbued with purpose, and inclined towards sin.[90]

---

[88] A. Scott Moreau, Evvy Hay Campbell, and Susan Greener, *Effective Intercultural Communication (Encountering Mission): A Christian Perspective*, 1st edition. (Grand Rapids, MI: Baker Academic, 2014).

[89] Moreau, Campbell, and Greener, *Effective Intercultural Communication (Encountering Mission)*, 230.

[90] Moreau, Campbell, and Greener, *Effective Intercultural Communication (Encountering Mission)*.

A Terminological and Paradigmatic Shift

Wan and Hedinger emphasize the necessity of a relationally oriented approach to intercultural interactions.[91] IRQ emerges as a distinct and crucial paradigm shift, emphasizing the relational dimension of intercultural communication and prioritizing the development of authentic, meaningful connections across cultures. IRQ reframes intercultural interactions and communication through the lens of relationships rather than as a competency to achieve. IRQ signifies more than just a new term in the field of intercultural communication or intercultural competency; it represents a fundamental paradigm shift from the traditional outcome-focused approaches of IC and ICC towards a more holistic and relationally based approach. This shift reflects a deeper understanding of intercultural communication, moving beyond the transactional and emphasizing the transformative power of intercultural relationships.

From Competence to Quotient

The shift from "competence" to "quotient" is deliberate and significant; while competence implies a set of acquired skills and knowledge, quotient suggests a capacity. This terminological change reflects a move away from a checklist approach to intercultural communication, acknowledging the fluid, dynamic, and deeply personal nature of intercultural relationships. Beyond the relational orientation of IRQ, this shift addresses the incongruency of measuring a subjective quality as a competence.[92] IRQ recognizes the subjectivity of intercultural relationships while also attempting to be accurate in the terminology used for its explanation.

From Outcomes to Relationships

The core distinction between IRQ and IC/ICC lies in the fundamental focus of each concept. While IC/ICC prioritize achieving specific communication goals and navigating cultural differences to achieve desired outcomes, IRQ centers on the cultivation and nurturing of authentic relationships as the foundation for meaningful intercultural communication and interactions. IRQ offers a distinctive framework for understanding intercultural

---

[91] Enoch Wan and Mark Hedinger, *Relational Missionary Training: Theology, Theory & Practice*, ed. Kendi Howells Douglas, Stephen Burris, and Jen Johnson (Urban Loft Publishers, 2020), 155.

[92] Karin Zotzmann, "The Impossibility of Defining and Measuring Intercultural Competencies," in *Resistance to the Known: Counter-Conduct in Language Education*, ed. Damian J. Rivers (London: Palgrave Macmillan UK, 2015), 168–91, https://doi.org/10.1057/9781137345196_8.

communication by shifting the focus from mere effectiveness to genuine connection. While traditional IC and ICC models prioritize achieving predetermined communication goals and minimizing misunderstandings, IRQ proposes a paradigm shift. It redefines success as the cultivation of meaningful relationships characterized by deep understanding, mutual transformation, and reciprocal growth. This shift necessitates a move away from viewing intercultural communication as primarily a skill-based endeavor, instead embracing it as an ongoing process of relational development.

IC and ICC models often aim to manage and control the inherent complexities of intercultural encounters, seeking predictable outcomes and minimizing potential for conflict, but IRQ embraces a different approach. IRQ recognizes the inherent complexity and ambiguity of intercultural encounters, encouraging individuals to view these as opportunities for growth, learning, and a more nuanced understanding of cultural differences. By acknowledging that discomfort and misunderstandings are inevitable aspects of intercultural engagement, IRQ empowers individuals to navigate these challenges constructively, fostering resilience and a deeper appreciation for the richness and value of cultural diversity. It is important to note that IRQ is not intended to replace or diminish the value of IC and ICC. Acquiring knowledge, skills, and behaviors are important for building intercultural relationships. Instead, IRQ offers a complementary perspective that enriches our understanding of intercultural communication by highlighting the crucial role of relationships in fostering genuine connection and understanding.

Aspects	Intercultural Competence	Intercultural Relational Quotient
Purpose	To learn and implement knowledge, skills, and behavior to effectively function in a different culture	To build relationships with beings from different cultures
Orientation	Programmatic, outcome-based	Relational
Perception	Solution (aka magic bullet)	Process of growth
Strategy	Transmission of knowledge, skills, behaviors	Interculturality
Scale	Micro	Micro, meso, and macro
Conceptualization of Culture	Static	Dynamic
Direction	Unidirectional	Multidirectional
Approach to Complexity	Seeks to manage and control uncertainty to achieve predictable outcomes	Embraces ambiguity and uncertainty as opportunities for growth and learning
Measure of Success	Achievement of communication goals, effective adaptation, and avoidance of misunderstandings	Quality of relationships, depth of understanding, and mutual transformation, extent of interaction across cultures

Aspects	Intercultural Competence	Intercultural Relational Quotient
Goal	Complete desired program outcomes and avoid misunderstandings	Cultivating authentic relationships and fostering genuine connection across cultures
Theological Perspective	Agnostic	Theologically Relational and Trinitarian

Figure 15. Comparison of Intercultural Competence and Intercultural Relational Quotient

As the table above illustrates, while both IC and IRQ aim to improve interactions between individuals from different cultures, intercultural competence and intercultural relational quotient differ significantly in their approach and ultimate goals. Intercultural competence emphasizes the acquisition of specific knowledge, skills, and behaviors deemed necessary to function effectively in a different culture. This approach is programmatic and outcome-based, often presented as a set of learnable steps, a process, or a checklist to achieve successful communication and adaptation. It perceives cultural interaction as a problem to be solved, with competence serving as the "magic bullet" to overcome cultural barriers and achieve predictable outcomes.

Strategies for developing intercultural competence often revolve around the transmission of knowledge, focusing on cultural differences and similarities, communication styles, and appropriate behaviors. This approach primarily operates on a micro level, focusing on individual interactions and skills. Culture is often viewed as a static entity, with an emphasis on understanding existing norms and practices. The direction of learning is typically unidirectional, from the individual seeking competence to the target culture. Success is measured by the achievement of communication goals, effective adaptation to the new cultural context, and the avoidance of misunderstandings.

In contrast, intercultural relational quotient prioritizes the cultivation of authentic relationships with individuals from different cultures. It emphasizes the relational aspect of intercultural interactions, recognizing that genuine connection requires more than just knowledge and skills. IRQ views intercultural engagement as a continuous process of growth, acknowledging the dynamic and evolving nature of culture.

Rather than seeking to manage and control uncertainty, IRQ embraces the complexity of intercultural relationships, focusing on the quality of connections, depth of understanding, and the potential for mutual transformation. IRQ operates on micro, meso, and macro levels, acknowledging the influence of societal structures and power dynamics on intercultural interactions. IRQ recognizes culture as a dynamic force, constantly shaped and reshaped by individual and collective experiences, promoting a multidirectional approach to learning, where all parties involved engage in a reciprocal exchange of knowledge, perspectives, and experiences. Ultimately, success in IRQ is measured by the quality of relationships, the depth of understanding achieved, the extent of mutual transformation experienced, and the frequency and depth of interactions across cultures. The goal is not merely successful communication but the fostering of genuine connection, empathy, and a shared sense of belonging across cultural boundaries.

Theoretical Understandings of IRQ in RICC

IRQ is naturally grounded within the framework of relational interactionism. This framework, highlighting the dynamic vertical relationships between the Trinity and individuals, as well as the horizontal relationships between people, provides a rich lens through which to understand the purpose and motivations driving the development of strong intercultural relationships. Through the lens of relational interactionism, the importance of IRQ becomes readily apparent. IRQ is not simply about acquiring a set of skills to function effectively or communicate a message in a culture; rather, it is about cultivating transformative relationships across boundaries through which both horizontal and vertical relationships are impacted.

IRQ and the relational interactionism framework emphasize the centrality of meaningful relationships in intercultural communication. Communication is not merely about transmitting information but about jointly constructing understanding through dialogue and shared experiences. Authentic intercultural relationships challenge our assumptions, broaden our perspectives, and foster personal growth. Relationships have the potential to be both transformational and transgressional. IRQ recognizes the self as inherently relational, shaped by and also shaping our interactions with others. This understanding challenges individualistic notions of communication, emphasizing the interconnectedness of individuals within a web of relationships.

Transformative and Transgressional Relationships

Authentic intercultural relationships challenge our assumptions, broaden our perspectives, and foster personal growth. IRQ has the potential to influence intercultural relationships in both positive and negative ways. Relationships have the potential to be both transformational and transgressional, according to Wan. As such, IRQ may impact the transformative or transgressional nature of relationships. Though no single factor could determine whether a relationship would be transformative or transgressional, higher IRQ would likely remove some barriers which might negatively impact the nature of a relationship. While the goal for relationships in intercultural contexts would be transformation for individuals, pointing and leading individuals to a closer relationship with Christ and the Trinity, the unfortunate reality is that there may be situations where transgressional relationships are at work and where relationships may not lead to the goal of greater unity and stronger relationships, neither vertically and horizontally.[93]

Cross-Cultural vs. Intercultural IRQ: A Two-Way Street

Within the context of intercultural interactions and IRQ, the differentiation between cross-cultural and intercultural can be illustrated through the analogy of one-way and two-way streets. IRQ in cross-cultural settings often reflects a one-sided adaptation, where individuals from one culture conform to a different culture's ways of interacting and communicating reciprocal learning and adaptation occurring by those in the other culture. In contrast, IRQ in intercultural settings emphasizes a two-way street, where individuals from different cultural backgrounds engage in a shared journey of understanding, respecting, and valuing each other's perspectives by both adapting and adjusting in order to navigate cultural barriers.

God-intelligence and Human-intelligence in RICC

The framework of relational interactionism necessitates understanding the role and impact of beings and Beings in RICC. In considering intercultural communication, two concepts may be helpful: God-intelligence and human-intelligence. God-intelligence (GI) refers to the divine guidance, revelation, and intervention that shapes understanding and prompts action, particularly in intercultural communication. GI involves God working in individuals' lives, often through supernatural means like visions, dreams, or strong impressions, to prepare them for intercultural encounters and to challenge their preconceived notions. GI precedes and lays the groundwork for the

---

[93] Wan and Raibley, *Transformational Change in Christian Ministry*, 28.

human component of communication. Human-intelligence (HI) encompasses the human capacity for understanding, responsiveness, and action within intercultural communication. HI pertains to individuals actively participating in the process of bridging cultural divides by demonstrating openness, receptivity, and a willingness to learn from others. HI follows as a result of GI, allowing individuals to act upon divine guidance and engage in meaningful cross-cultural interactions.

The account of Peter and Cornelius in Acts 10 provides a powerful illustration of how God uses both GI and HI to orchestrate intercultural understanding and expand the reach of the Gospel. This narrative, centered on the deeply ingrained ethnocentricity of the early Jewish church, reveals a process of transformation that moves from an individual to a community, the Jerusalem church. Peter, a prominent leader of the Jerusalem church, was deeply shaped by his Jewish upbringing and the prevailing cultural norms that separated Jews from Gentiles. His initial resistance to engaging with Cornelius, a Gentile Roman centurion, highlights the powerful influence of cultural conditioning.

However, God, in His wisdom, orchestrated a series of events to challenge Peter's ethnocentricity and reveal His heart for all people. Peter's vision in Joppa (Acts 10:9-16), repeated three times for emphasis, directly confronted his cultural biases. The symbolism of the vision, involving animals considered unclean by Jewish law, underscored the need for a radical shift in perspective. This divine intervention, a clear example of GI, prepared Peter's heart for the unexpected invitation from Cornelius. The timing of the vision, coinciding with Cornelius' own divine prompting from God (Acts 10:1-8), reveals the meticulous orchestration of the Holy Spirit, working in both the Jewish and Gentile contexts.

Cornelius, described as a devout and God-fearing Gentile (Acts 10:2), exemplifies openness to God's leading. His immediate obedience to the angel's instruction to summon Peter (Acts 10:3-8) demonstrates his faith and willingness to cross cultural boundaries. Unlike Peter, who grappled with cultural prejudices, Cornelius exhibited a remarkable readiness to receive God's message, regardless of its source.

Peter's encounter with Cornelius led to a profound transformation in his understanding of the Gospel. He recognized that God shows no partiality (Acts 10:34) and that salvation is available to all who believe in Jesus Christ. This realization, a result of both GI and his own growing HI, empowered Peter to share the Gospel with boldness, leading to Cornelius' conversion and the outpouring of the Holy Spirit on his household (Acts 10:44-48).

The impact of Peter's experience extended beyond his personal transformation. His subsequent defense of his actions before the skeptical

Jewish believers in Jerusalem (Acts 11:1-18) marked a crucial step in the church's journey toward embracing its multiethnic identity. The outpouring of the Holy Spirit on Cornelius' household, mirroring the Pentecost experience, served as undeniable evidence of God's acceptance of the Gentiles. This event sparked a process of communal transformation, culminating in the Jerusalem Council, where the church officially recognized the inclusion of Gentiles. The transition, however, was not without its challenges, highlighting the persistent influence of ethnocentricity even within the Christian community.

IRQ and the Relational Intercultural Communication Paradigm

The capacity to cultivate meaningful intercultural relationships is significantly impacted by an individual's IRQ, with this influence particularly evident within the framework of the Relational Intercultural Communication (RICC) paradigm.

IRQ in Being

As the RICC paradigm is not strictly sequential but rather cyclical, the *being* stage is not isolated as the first step. However, this stage draws more heavily upon an individual's self-awareness and understanding of their own cultural framework rather than on interactions between individuals. For an individual to grow in their IRQ capacity, they must first have the foundational awareness of their culture or cultures. As such, while the *being* stage creates a foundation for fruitful intercultural interactions and communication by first considering the individual. The greater an individual's IRQ, the more they are able to interact and build relationships with those from other cultures. Recognizing the influence of cultural patterns that feel normal to an individual is essential. These ingrained patterns, often unconscious, shape communication styles, social interactions, and interpretations of behavior. By growing in awareness of one's own being, individuals are then better able to navigate the cultural differences that they encounter with sensitivity and respect.

Individuals with lower IRQ may operate from a place of unconscious incompetence, unaware of how their own cultural biases color their perceptions and interactions. This can lead to misinterpretations, strained communication, and difficulty forming genuine connections with individuals from different cultural backgrounds. Conversely, higher IRQ fosters cultural sensitivity and the ability to recognize one's own cultural lens, promoting empathy and understanding in intercultural encounters.

IRQ in Belonging

Building upon the foundation of being, the *belonging* stage focuses on the construction of bridges that connect individuals across cultural divides. These bridges manifest in various forms, encompassing shared worldviews, aligned thought patterns, and mutually understood languages, both verbal and nonverbal. Effective intercultural communication requires a conscious effort to bridge differences in worldview, recognizing that cultural perspectives shape interpretations of reality, values, and beliefs. Aligning thought patterns involves understanding and adapting to diverse cognitive styles, such as linear versus holistic thinking, to facilitate mutual comprehension. Language, both verbal and nonverbal, serves as the primary tool for communication, and bridging linguistic differences, including nuances in meaning and cultural context, is crucial. Furthermore, recognizing the influence of social structures, media consumption, and desired outcomes on communication patterns is essential for building strong and lasting intercultural relationships.

Lower IRQ can hinder this process, as individuals may struggle to decode diverse communication styles, rely on stereotypes, and experience anxiety when navigating unfamiliar cultural landscapes. This can lead to superficial interactions and a limited capacity for building genuine intercultural relationships. However, higher IRQ equips individuals with the tools and mindset to navigate cultural complexities, adapt their communication style, and engage in meaningful dialogue that transcends cultural barriers, fostering a sense of belonging for both themselves and others.

IRQ in Becoming

The transformative potential of RICC finds its fullest expression in the *becoming* stage, where individual growth intersects with broader societal implications. This stage aligns with the teleological goal articulated in Revelation 7:9, envisioning a unified and diverse body of believers from every nation, tribe, people, and language. Within the context of intercultural communication, this vision translates into celebrating cultural differences and building relationships characterized by trust, understanding, and empathy. Furthermore, *becoming* aligns with the missiological goals of *missio Dei* – God's mission – which emphasizes God's love for all people and the call for reconciliation and justice throughout creation. Cultivating IRQ, therefore, becomes not merely a personal endeavor but a spiritual imperative, contributing to a more just and compassionate world that reflects the diversity and unity of God's kingdom.

Individuals with lower IRQ may view cultural differences as obstacles rather than opportunities for enrichment, limiting their engagement with other cultures and hindering their personal growth. However, those with higher IRQ have a genuine appreciation for cultural diversity, recognizing God's character reflected in the diversity of cultures, seeking out intercultural experiences, learning from others, and challenging their own cultural perspectives. This, in turn, contributes to a more inclusive and harmonious society where intercultural relationships are valued and celebrated.

IRQ and Processes of Intercultural Communication

IRQ impacts communication within intercultural contexts, drawing upon the provided definition of communication as a continuum of internal and external processes involving perception, conception, volition and expression. By examining how IRQ impacts each stage of this continuum, we can gain a deeper understanding of its crucial role in fostering effective and meaningful intercultural interactions. Interactive Relational Communication posits that effective intercultural engagement hinges not only on observable behaviors but also on the intricate processes that shape our understanding. This section delves into how IRQ profoundly impacts the internal and external processes – perception, conception, and discernment/decision – fostering more nuanced and empathetic intercultural understanding.

Perception: Beyond Cultural Filters to Relational Acuity

Perception, the foundational stage of communication, involves how individuals perceive and interpret stimuli from their environment. However, these perceptions are not objective; they are inevitably filtered through our cultural lenses, shaping our understanding of the world around us. Individuals with higher IRQ, recognizing the pervasive influence of these cultural filters, cultivate a heightened awareness of both their own cultural biases and those of others. This heightened awareness allows individuals to move beyond ethnocentric interpretations, acknowledging that their own cultural framework is not the sole lens through which to interpret the world.

For instance, a person with low IRQ might misinterpret a direct communication style as aggressive, based on their own cultural norms valuing indirectness. Conversely, someone with high IRQ, understanding the cultural basis for directness, would perceive it as a sign of honesty and respect within that specific cultural context. This nuanced understanding, rooted in cultural sensitivity and empathy, allows for more accurate and less biased perception of communicative cues. IRQ differs from intercultural competency in this scenario through its underlying relational motivation.

Conception/Interpretation: Navigating Diverse Meaning-Making Systems with Cognitive Empathy

Once a stimulus is perceived, the next stage involves conception, where individuals draw upon their cultural knowledge and experiences to make sense of the perceived information. This meaning-making process is inherently cultural, as different cultures possess distinct ways of interpreting the world, organizing information, and attributing meaning to events.

IRQ influences how individuals recognize the inherent diversity in meaning-making systems and approach intercultural communication with a posture of humility, understanding that their own cultural meaning-making processes are not exhaustive. In this conception/interpretation stage, IRQ allows individuals to move beyond their own interpretations to acknowledge and understand the interpretations of those with discrete meaning-making systems. For instance, an individual with high IRQ might come to one interpretation of a Scripture passage but would be able to understand how someone from a different culture came to a different but equally valid interpretation from their meaning-making system.

Volition: Choosing Respectful Engagement through Ethical Consciousness

The final stage involves the conscious decision of how to respond to the perceived stimulus. This is where IRQ plays a crucial role in shaping communication choices that are both effective and culturally sensitive. Individuals with high IRQ are more likely to choose communication strategies that demonstrate respect, empathy, and a willingness to bridge cultural differences.

This might manifest in various ways:

- **Active Listening:** Paying close attention to both verbal and nonverbal cues, asking clarifying questions, and demonstrating genuine interest in understanding the other person's perspective.
- **Perspective-Taking:** Making a conscious effort to see the situation from the other person's point of view, considering their cultural background, experiences, and values.
- **Code-Switching:** Adapting one's communication style to align with the cultural norms of the other person, while remaining authentic to oneself.
- **Patience and Understanding:** Recognizing that intercultural communication can be challenging and requires patience, persistence, flexibility, and a willingness to accept ambiguity.

The impact of IRQ on the processes of intercultural communication can significantly impact the course of intercultural relationships. By fostering relational acuity in perception, promoting cognitive empathy in conception, and encouraging intercultural consciousness in decision-making, IRQ empowers individuals to move beyond understanding intercultural dynamics for a specific goal towards a more nuanced and reciprocal posture of learning, engaging, and interacting with those from other cultures. This shift, from egocentric to ethnorelative,[94] from judgment to understanding, holds the potential to create intercultural encounters which are not merely opportunities for navigating differences but rather catalysts for building bridges of genuine connection and shared humanity.

Developing IRQ for Greater RICC

Wan's multidimensional definition of interculturality, while eschewing an evaluative framework, offers valuable markers for understanding the progressive development of IRQ. These dimensions provide a roadmap for individuals seeking to cultivate deeper intercultural understanding and engagement. As individuals progress towards higher IRQ, they demonstrate increasing proficiency across these dimensions. These dimensions serve as interconnected and mutually reinforcing aspects of IRQ, offering individuals tangible areas for growth as they strive towards greater interculturality.

Interculturality

Wan defines interculturality as "both the commitment and competence of someone venturing beyond his/her cultural background and boundary with multidimensional qualities, such as self-identity (psychological), multiculturality (ideational), intentionality (attitudinal) and practicality (operational)."[95] As Wan's definition details, interculturality has four aspects: self-identity, multiculturality, intentionality, and practicality. These are multidimensional qualities which can gauge an individual's interculturality. In many ways, interculturality can be considered in a similar manner to a growth mindset or progression in which an individual grows in intercultural abilities, capabilities, attitudes, and tendencies. While it is difficult to evaluate or quantitatively measure an individual's interculturality, this concept provides great value in terms of intercultural education for educators and teachers.

---

[94] Sonia Chan, "A Relational Model of Intercultural Learning and Interactions," in *Transformational Change in Christian Ministry*, ed. Enoch Wan and Jon Raibley (Western Academic Publishers, 2022), 178.

[95] Enoch Wan, Mark Hedinger, and Jon Raibley, *Relational Intercultural Education for Intercultural Ministry* (Portland, OR: Western Academic Publishers, 2024), 4.

Interculturality can be considered as a continuum that can be pursued both by individuals and within a curriculum. For learners, interculturality can be both learned and experienced within learning communities and within educational settings. Interculturality is a holistic approach to intercultural interactions, as it takes into consideration psychological, ideational, attitudinal, and operational aspects. This may sound similar to many intercultural competency models which use behavioral, skills based, knowledge based and attitudinal components to measure intercultural competence. However, interculturality is founded in and based on relational interactionism, which shifts the focus from outcome-based objectives to relationships.

Rather than being a linear progression or a step-by-step map to perfect interculturality, interculturality is much more of a holistic and cyclical process by which both transformative and transgressional change can be affected. As such, the different qualities that influence and impact each other as an individual grows in one aspect will likely influence the other qualities. Similarly, if transgressional change occurs and a quality is reduced in an individual, that will likely also impact the other qualities in that individual. Interculturality can be considered on micro, meso, and macro levels in terms of intercultural interactions. However, in the context of intercultural education, likely the micro and meso levels are most involved.

The multidimensional qualities of interculturality as defined by Wan, while not evaluative, provide helpful markers as individuals develop greater interculturality through IRQ.[96] Each quality will be discussed briefly below as it relates to a multiethnic theology of ethnicity and its practical implications:

Self-Identity (psychological): A multiethnic theology encourages individuals to examine their thoughts, assumptions, and biases to recognize the cultural filters that may shape and color their interactions. Greater self-awareness in this area allows individuals to then respond in more culturally contextualized ways. This process of self-reflection, rooted in humility and a willingness to learn, is crucial for intercultural interactions.

Multiculturality (ideational): Moving beyond the initial recognition of different cultures, a multiethnic theology of ethnicity emphasizes appreciating and valuing all different ethnicities and cultures. By doing so, one develops genuine curiosity and a willingness to learn from other perspectives.

Intentionality (attitudinal): A multiethnic theology challenges individuals to move beyond tolerance to active engagement with diverse ethnicities. This

---

[96] Wan, Hedinger, and Raibley, *Relational Intercultural Education for Intercultural Ministry*, 4.

may require an attitude or perspective shift as it impacts an individual's approach to other ethnicities and cultures. Ultimately, intentionality moves an individual from thoughts into action.

Practicality (operational): A multiethnic theology translates into visible actions. Individuals are motivated to develop relationships and learn from others for fruitful intercultural interactions. Barriers to communication and relationships are overcome with respect, understanding, intentional work, and unity in Christ.

These qualities of interculturality cannot be isolated from each other; they integrate in a holistic manner, with each influencing and impacting the others. Rather than being a step-by-step or sequential progression, these qualities of interculturality can increase or decrease in individuals in any order. However, as one changes, it is likely that the others will fluctuate in a similar manner. Interculturality is not a set scale which has a completion mark; as such, interculturality cannot be something that is pursued and then checked off once mastery is achieved. Instead, it is a continual lifelong pursuit, in which individuals are ideally ever-expanding in their capacity for interculturality as they develop in self-identity, multiculturality, intentionality, and practicality with intercultural interactions.

IRQ in Intercultural Contexts

For IRQ to have significant impact, it must move beyond theory to be both practical and applicable. The following list highlights a few contexts where IRQ has the potential to play a vital role in intercultural interactions and communication:

- Intercultural Education: Educators with greater IRQ are better equipped to create learning communities and environments that respect and value the diverse backgrounds of their students. They can facilitate meaningful dialogue, bridge cultural gaps, and empower students to learn from each other, while encouraging greater IRQ among students.
- Multicultural Churches: IRQ enables church leaders and members to move beyond superficial tolerance towards genuine understanding and appreciation of different cultural behaviors and attitudes, including expressions of faith. This fosters unity, encourages authentic relationships, and strengthens the church's outreach within diverse communities. IRQ also impacts a church's theology on ethnicity and subsequently their embodiment of this theology.
- Intercultural Missions: Missionaries with great IRQ are able to build trust, show respect, and communicate the message of the Gospel in a culturally sensitive and relevant manner. By understanding the

values, beliefs, and communication styles of the target culture, missionaries can build genuine relationships and share their faith in ways that resonate with the local community.

In these contexts and beyond, IRQ is paramount for breaking down barriers, fostering empathy, and building bridges of understanding across cultures. The development of IRQ is not merely a pragmatic skill, but rather a profound expression of the Christian call to live in unity and love.

Conclusion

IRQ emphasizes the importance of building meaningful connections and fostering genuine understanding between individuals from different cultural backgrounds. Unlike traditional approaches focused on competence and communication outcomes, IRQ prioritizes the relational dimensions of intercultural engagement. It represents a paradigm shift towards a more holistic, relationship-centered approach to intercultural communication. By examining how IRQ impacts the internal processes of perception, conception, and decision-making, we can gain a deeper understanding of its role in facilitating intercultural understanding. IRQ enables individuals to move beyond cultural filters, cultivating heightened awareness of their own and others' biases. Grounded in relational interactionism, IRQ is not just about acquiring skills, but about cultivating transformative relationships across cultural boundaries. Ultimately, IRQ guides individuals to choose communication strategies that demonstrate respect, empathy, and a willingness to bridge cultural differences, promoting transformative intercultural relationships. Developing IRQ is essential for fostering genuine cross-cultural understanding and collaboration in today's globalized world.

CHAPTER 6
Relational Communication for Relational Education: Part I

COMMUNICATING ACROSS CULTURAL BARRIERS

Relational Communication in the Context of Relational Intercultural Education

The value of any model is tested by its ability to give insight into practical, real-world situations. This chapter will use the model of RICC as presented in chapter 3 and IRQ as seen in Chapter 4 with application to educational situations.

Figure 16 graphically presents the practical application of RICC, a communication model, as it is seen in intercultural education. It is worth noting that Figure 16 could easily be modified to show practical application of RICC to many other fields, for example intercultural leadership, intercultural medicine, or intercultural business.

Figure 16 begins with the recognition that God is active in education, just as in all other phases of life. An encouraging reminder comes from Matthew 28:20. Even though we often limit that verse to "great commission" sending of missionaries, in fact the promise of that verse includes all levels of education: teaching them to obey all that Christ has commanded and resting in the promise of His presence exactly in that same context. God is present and He leads us as we teach His Word to people from any generation, national background, or language.

Figure 16 goes beyond that vertical relationship of God and people to also include the horizontal interaction between two people, each surrounded by their own community. The horizontal lines that connect the two members of this communication dyad are represented by the larger stick figures, person a and person b.

Between a and b we have cyclical lines of expression and perception. Expression refers to the verbal and nonverbal signals that a person uses to communicate to the world outside. Perception refers to the phase of communication by which we receive stimuli from the outside world; some of that stimuli we receive at face value, but our perceptions are always shaped by our internal world of previous experiences and cultural conditioning. Much of the stimuli we receive gets ignored or re-imagined according to our previous experiences and the expectations that we hold.

At the sides of Figure 16, we also have the phases of communication that we refer to as conception (how we think of a message) and volition (our willful decision about how to respond to a message). These two phases of communication are internal; they take place within a person in response to the message that was perceived (which may or may not have been an accurate reflection of the intended message expressed by our dyad partner). The result of these internal processes leads to another "expression" (as seen in Fig 16) which of course person b will perceive in a continuation of the cycle of communication.

In Figure 16, we have represented the two exterior phases of communication (perception and expression) as horizontal lines that connect person "a" with person "b". What person "a" expresses becomes the perception phase for person "b" and what person "b" expresses becomes the perception phase for person "a".

Within a given cultural setting, the likelihood is that a given educational context will be marked by a mostly shared understanding of words, concepts, goals, methods, and motivations. The assumption within a given culture is that what a teacher expresses and what a learner perceives are at least approximately the same.

When we enter the realm of intercultural education, we recognize the additional challenges to perception by all parties involved. We anticipate that there will be misunderstandings or areas where intended meanings may not align with perceived meanings. Perceptions of a given message may be widely divergent between person a and person b based on such educational factors as:

- The **educational structure** (formal, nonformal, informal)
- The **educational setting** (home-based, church-based, school-based, internet-based).
- The **educational topic, scope and sequence** (a short video posted online to show how to bake one recipe of cookies compared to a four-year residential degree in culinary arts).
- The **educational outcomes** (cognitive/affective/behavioral outcomes named vs a simple demonstration without any claims of expected outcomes, for example).
- The **educational methods** (lecture, demonstration, experience-based education, group dialog, reflective consideration, active experimentation etc.).
- The **language of education** (both the difference in delivery language and the register and/or technical vocabulary used).
- **Educational relationships** (is a healthy learner/teacher relationship reflected by a level of closeness between learner and teacher? Or is strict separation and formality expected?)

- **Educational leadership** (is it appropriate for learners to raise questions and suggest alternative ideas? Or is the word of the professor to be accepted without challenge?)

These factors are, in essence, the prisms as seen in Figure 16.

It seems that nearly every school that offers intercultural studies will include a specialty course in intercultural education. This list of areas where perceptions vary helps to explain why that is. There are so many variables that differ from one culture to another; so many opportunities for the perceptions of learners from one culture to be widely different from the intended expression of the teacher or facilitator who comes from a different culture.

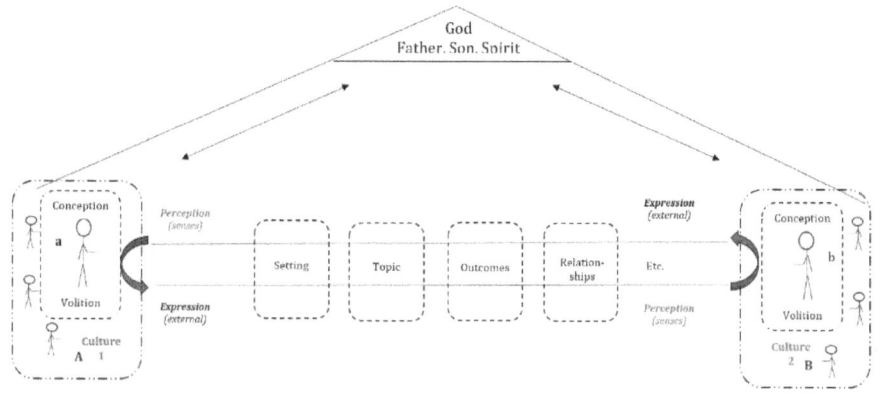

Figure 16. Relational Communication in Intercultural Education
(See Figure 7)

Figure 16 is a modification of the original Figure 7, now making it clear that perceptions will vary depending on a wide range of educational variables. Intercultural educational practitioners will be aware of these variables and will take steps to understand the expectations of their learners across all the possible chasms. In Figure 16 we will call those different variables "perception prisms." Similar to how a prism separates light into component wavelengths, so these educational variables will separate perceptions about education into component elements. So, the teacher whose preference is teaching in a coffee shop may need to find connection with a student who prefers a classroom with white board and teaching lectern. How do you bridge that gap? Somehow there will be common ground by finding the "common components" between the classroom and the coffeeshop so that the educational relationship can develop.

I recently heard a story of a teacher who found it difficult to work with students in her host culture. The cultural norm was that people were free to come and go at any time in this culture. This cultural norm extended to the classroom, and this teacher's educational situation was such that it felt appropriate for students to come and go at any moment. You can imagine that this made it difficult for a teacher who came from a different background.

One of the other activities at this educational setting was horseback riding. The teacher realized that even though a particular area of content was not grasped well in a classroom where people came and went, students would stay in the saddle for a horse ride. The teacher found ways to introduce her content while she and the students were on their horses. The "common components" between the classroom and the horseback sessions proved to be sufficient in that case, and a bridge was built across the cultural gap.

Many approaches to intercultural education take that list of perception prisms and build a catalog of issues within each of them. That catalog, then, becomes the basis for teaching intercultural education. This approach teaches the existence of such social phenomenon as individualism/collectivism, power distance, or honor/shame to describe the cultures with which we are working.

That approach, fascinating as it is, will not ultimately lead to fruitful intercultural education. As anyone in intercultural studies has experienced, there are scores of social science theories that explain one bit of intercultural life or another. There is a certain truth to all of that, and it is useful to know the insights that scholars, researchers, and intercultural practitioners have developed.[97] Their contributions are significant in helping us cognitively understand what varies from one culture to another. But interactive relational intercultural education requires more than understanding at that cognitive level. Connecting across cultures starts with recognition of the wide variety of those "perception prisms" but it goes further; it requires the practitioner to build bridges that cross those differences so that perceptions begin to approximate intentions. It is that practical side of "how do we build a bridge" that makes us suggest a relational interactive approach to intercultural education.

The Intercultural Relational Quotient idea presented in Chapter 4 gives us a better model for considering the cultural gaps that disrupt healthy relational patterns between people of differing cultural backgrounds. Within that IRQ concept we find some issues that are "perception-based," some that are "receptor-based," some that are cognitive, others that are volitional. As we consider those various "prisms," there is no standard formula for

---

[97] We refer here to authors such as Hofstede, Trompenaars, Meyer, Lingenfelter, Plueddemann, Wu, Georges, Deardorff, etc.

intercultural competency. Rather, what we have is a mixture of elements to consider in any specific context. Interculturality is both art and science: it clearly includes some specific cultural elements, but how those elements should interact varies from one relational context to another.

Communication within Intercultural Education: An Interactive Relational Approach

Returning to Figure 16 we recognize communication in four phases: perception, conception, volition, and expression. Chapter three went into detail about these four phases in a discussion of Intercultural Communication. Now we want to take those same four phases and consider them in light of relational interactive education.

In a previous volume, Wan, Hedinger and Raibley[98] developed the idea of Interactive Relational Intercultural Education (RICE). The outcome of that study is that interactive relational education revolves around the three themes of being, belonging and becoming. We will consider communication in light of that educational model.

By building on the being-belonging-becoming perspective, we move from a static view of cultural variables to a relational view of dynamic interaction between people whose "being" may start at different cultural points but who develop and grow together toward becoming something different than they were. The interactive dynamic process does not leave practitioners where they were; and it also does not simply add knowledge to that previous state. It takes knowledge of the original state of 'being' and adds to that an interactive, dynamic relationship which teaches deeply through whole-person experience and involvement, eventually leading to becoming a different person, one who interacts with another person who is also growing and developing.

---

[98] Wan, Hedinger, and Raibley, *Relational Intercultural Education for Intercultural Ministry*.

Process / Interaction	Being	Belonging	Becoming	Educational illustration
Perception Person 1 and 2	The starting point is monocultural perception by both learner and facilitator across many of the perceptual prisms	A growing interaction with one or a few people from another culture leads to recognition and identification of differences in educational expectations	By interacting in different contexts, activities, discussions, etc. persons 1 and 2 develop a way to discuss and learn from one another; perceptions by person 1 grow closer to the intended meaning of person 2.	Teachers help learners to perceive what is important in their area of study; Learning to observe and distinguish one thing from another.
Conception Person 1 and 2	At first, the content is likely misunderstood by learner because of misperceptions about the nature and content of teaching.	Content conception and Process conception – both the learner and the teacher begin to learn the others' approach to life (process conception). With growing understanding of one another, there is also increased grasp of the content of the teaching.	Together growing in understanding the content of the education as well as the cultural expectations of all involved. This leads to becoming bicultural in education; able to shift from educational preferences of one culture to the educational preferences of the other culture.	Teachers & learners from different cultures may differ in their thought patterns. A good result of becoming is both teacher & learner growing in reciprocity of their educational approaches.

Process Interaction	Being	Belonging	Becoming	Educational illustration
Volition Person 1 and 2	People who do well in RICC have character qualities of humility, curiosity, willingness to be corrected (teachability), flexibility, acceptance of ambiguity and respect for people from other cultural backgrounds. These character elements are present even before entering the intercultural context.	Engaging in interactive relationship by teachers & learners requires the will to: Be humble to accept correction, Be aware of errors in under- standing, be curious about the ways of life of other people, and deeply respect the others in the educational setting. Interaction with these character traits permits increased learning of both content and the interactive relationship that crosses cultural gaps.	By engaging in interactive relationship with people from other cultures, the teacher and learner are both given the opportunity to grow as individuals and to increasingly appreciate the other members of the relationship. This level of volition ends up permitting learning within other cultural patterns as well; to him who has, more will be given.	Teaching & learning both require the volitional will to work through differences in under- standing until learning objectives are accomplished. The work requires a will.

Process / Interaction	Being	Belonging	Becoming	Educational illustration
Expression Person 1 and 2	Early in the relationship, expressions to people from other cultures grow from monocultural experiences. In Bennett's[99] terms, the "denial" level of ethnocentric response that naively assumes all cultures are the same.	Interacting across cultures creates a "belonging" relationship that recognizes multiple ways to face life issues, and shows how those alternatives are legitimate.	A bicultural person who expresses himself appropriately within various cultural contexts. This grows from 1 – knowing how cultures work 2 – skill in culture learning 3 – volitional response of being willing to learn 4 – relationships through which to learn.	Ethnocentrism is replaced by ethno-relativism through personal interaction with people from other cultures.
IRQ	Learners and teachers at low IRQ because of lack of intercultural experience	Human interactions + will + God's influence	Increased IRQ	Inter-culturality increasing both vertically and horizontally

Figure 17. Being, Belonging, Becoming and Communication[100]

Figure 17 merges together three main themes in our study. The table ties together

---

[99] Milton Bennett, DMIS
[100] "Be aware of errors in understanding" in figure above from Stanislas Dehaene, *How We Learn: Why Brains Learn Better Than Any Machine... for Now* (Penguin Books, 2020).

1) The educational pathway for personal growth and transformation (as seen in the dynamic being-belonging-becoming progression)
2) The pathway for communication within educational contexts (seen in the perception-conception-volition-expression cycle)
3) The qualitative importance of IRQ as a mixture of multiple intercultural elements which are present within the people who are involved in this intercultural educational relationship.

So far in this chapter we have considered a relational interaction based on two individuals. This dyad perspective is helpful for developing the model and is also helpful for the individual teacher who is working with an individual student/learner. Such modeling is helpful to see the being-belonging-becoming concept worked out in terms of intercultural relational communication and education.

But most of the time, interactions between cultures in real life situations include groups of people more than simply two individuals. For the remainder of this chapter, we will consider communication issues that occur when interactions across cultures include groups of people.

Figure 16 will be our guide for this discussion. In Figure 16, the lower-case a and b refer to individuals (much like Figure 7). Capital letters in Figure 16 refer to groups of people who share common cultural patterns. The communication that occurs between A and B refers, then, to group interactions.

At one level, the perception-conception-volition-expression interactions remain the same for a/b dyad as for the A/B interactions. There are still perceptions that may or may not accurately reflect the intention of the speaker. There are still thought processes, willful attitude processes, and decisions that are expressed between the larger groups.

What is quite different, though, is the in-group communication that is inevitably occurring even while the intercultural communication is taking place. One cycle of communication is taking place within a group of people even while that group is engaging people from another culture. That cycle at once recognizes the presence of the intercultural conversation, and also tends to confirm the position of the group as a whole.

An illustration is helpful. In medical interpreting, the interpreter is trained to facilitate the conversation between patient and provider. If the interpreter takes on his or her own "persona" it will almost inevitably result in two people "against" one at some point. The points of interaction could be in terms of provider/patient relationship (for instance, if the provider insists on a first name basis while the patient prefers a more high-power distance relationship). It could also be in terms of a treatment plan where the doctor is soliciting the input of the patient to know what lifestyle changes are likely to be followed, while the patient is requesting a more directive set of "doctor's orders." At any rate, if there are two people in discussion, they will have to discuss and decide on their own. An interpreter should facilitate that conversation without injecting opinions.

But what if the interpreter does inject opinions? Now there are "two" on one side of the discussion and "one" on the other. The nature of the conversation changes and one likely result is that the discussion will not be based on the merits of each argument, but on the social pressure being exerted. The one is more likely to "cave in" to the two but not for the reasons that will lead to good medical outcomes.

In-group dynamics amid an intercultural debate have the same effect. Rather than lead to clearer communication of the intentions of the people involved, these in-group conversations can often create "us vs. them" mentalities which undermine good communication. Perceptions are reinforced, accepted ways of thinking are reinforced, volitional reactions toward the other group are muted as each group favors its own group cohesion instead of wishing to bridge to the other group, and expressions within the cycle of communication are less interested in bridge-building and more interested in maintaining the in-group cohesion and *status quo*.

In essence, what happens internally in the a/b dyad now happens "internally" in the discussions within the in-group. Opinions, expressions of volition, perceptions are voiced but only within the safety of the "in group."

Returning to our educational context, let us consider how this intercultural communication dynamic occurs within group interactions. We will look at a case study of an individual missionary teacher working with students and faculty who come from their own relatively homogeneous in-group.

In this case, a missionary teacher is living and working with a group of students and a group of other teachers, all from a host nation different from the missionary's. The students have a common language and basically common view of the education that they are receiving. They have a shared perception of the missionary teacher. It is shared not only because of their own shared backgrounds, but also because they talk about it! Outside of class, there is a steady flow of joking about the funny accent and discussion about ideas that were not "expressed" well (in fact, which were not perceived well, but the group will almost always shift the responsibility to the teacher instead of asking if they might have misunderstood the intended message). Students will do the work that this teacher requires, but with an attitude that is far short of fully engaged learners. They are interested in the material and motivated to advance in their studies, but they react negatively to the perceived shortcomings of the teacher.

At some point, the scenario just described results in a crisis of some sort. Perhaps the teacher errs in how much homework can be tolerated over a weekend. Perhaps there is a national holiday that is not respected as it should be. Perhaps there is a difficult emotional event – an accident perhaps, or a student who must leave to take care of family during an emergency. In these cases, that simmering perception of a teacher who is unengaged will result in either an open conflict or in the coldness of broken relationship.

The events just described come from my own story, as a young teacher from the United States teaching at a school in Latin America. I learned the hard way the importance of "belonging" within the group so that I might "become" a more accepted and more trustworthy part of the community. The cost of not belonging was that I did not understand the misperceptions that were being accepted, and when that crisis time did occur (as it always will, sooner or later), the rift between students of one culture and teacher of another was substantial. It was really another school year and input from trusted insiders from that culture that allowed me to start identifying and dealing with misperceptions.

The misperceptions were present because that is normal, natural human behavior. The group will support its own conception of what is occurring, and difficulties will be attributed to the perceived shortcomings of the expat. It was when I began to seek out the help and advice of a small group of faculty members from within the nation that I finally began to learn, to "hear" through their ears, and eventually to "become" a trusted member of the teaching staff.

That communication cycle points to an important question. Why did the expat teacher not more fully engage with the cultural patterns at the beginning? What were the causes that kept him from belonging?

Cross cultural relationships are complex. In this case, there are issues of volition, expression, conception and perception.

Learning to belong to a new culture requires a new set of perceptions and expressions. It is a difficult process and it is easier to simply avoid moving in that direction. It takes involvement in activities that do not feel natural. It requires learning to eat foods, keep schedules, and go about activities in ways that do not follow the normal patterns of one's homeland. Learning to belong in an unfamiliar culture requires being open to correction when one makes a mis-step, correction which adults really dislike. Learning to belong within a culture that is not your own is enormously challenging at levels of will, of cognition, of behavior. It is just easier to avoid that. Many expats form small communities that maintain their homelands' patterns of life. But avoiding the patterns of the host culture results in a ministry that is weakened. Without "belonging" there is very little chance of "becoming" a contributing member of that new cultural group. This clearly brings to view the issue of volition. One must have the will to face the challenges of engaging with an unfamiliar culture.

But it is not only a matter of will. The knowledge that there are different patterns of communication is a cognitive element involved in "belonging." Until someone begins to recognize different forms of speech, behavior, thought and relationship, it is unlikely that they will be able to adjust to those differences. These cognitive "facts" are reflected in the ability to perceive what was intended from a given cross-cultural exchange, and then appropriately respond.

As we consider this case study, it is critically important to return to the vertical relationship, or what Hannah Kappler's chapter calls, "God Intelligence." Why could Paul say that he had learned to be all things to all men (1 Cor 9:19-23)? Paul, as any human, had to go through these same difficulties of learning to communicate well with a group of people from a culture very different from his own. In Paul's case, we can see the vertical relationship that was a significant part of shaping his perceptions, conceptions, volition and expression.

Acts 17:16 - 33 provides a case study of how Paul learned to be all things to all people. We can trace the "being-belonging-becoming" pattern through this chapter and see how the vertical relationship with God was central to Paul's learning to "belong."

Being: Paul began as a strict Jew, avoiding all that would leave one ceremonially unclean. He also would have been very involved with Jewish writings but not so deeply involved with the writings of other people.

Belonging: The Lord engaged Paul in many occasions, but for our purposes we will highlight two narratives, one from Acts 9 and the other from Acts 17.

In Acts 9, God's vertical relationship with Saul led to his salvation and such a deep transformation that he changed his name to Paul. The miracle of three days without sight led to a new community for Paul: a new "belonging" within the young church. Saul became Paul and the former persecutor of the church became an outspoken defender of the faith as he belonged to the growing Christian community starting with Ananias, growing to the disciples from Damascus, and from there to Barnabus. The belonging that Saul experienced led to becoming the man who could say that he became all things to all people that by all means he could reach some.

In Acts 17 there is another narrative of Paul's life. In this chapter we see Paul in dialog with the Athenians, quoting their poets and declaring Christ to them through their own arts and temples and writers. This is the sort of "belonging" that opened doors for the gospel. Without in any way denying his relationship with the True God, Paul was able to enter into the life of the

Athenians to build enough of a bridge of mutual belonging that he could then introduce them to the "God in whom we live and move and have our being" (Acts 17:26). In that exchange, Paul continued to explain and introduce the God of the Bible, leading to the conversion of at least two people – Dionysius and Damaris (17:34).

Being-belonging-becoming is more than a horizontal pattern. God works vertically through it as well; starting with Saul as he was, a persecutor of the church. From being, God put Paul into a community of "becoming" where he began to understand the gospel and also to understand more of the gentile nations around them. In that context of belonging, God used Paul to establish the church and bring many people into the Kingdom of God. Paul could see all of that in his own life, realizing that he could become all things to all men so that some might become new creatures in Christ.

Conclusion

Individual a/b dyad analysis shows how a communication cycle of perception-conception-volition-expression interacts with relational interaction as seen in the being-belonging-becoming paradigm. When individuals enter into Relational Interactive Communication, there are opportunities for both to grow into something new as they interact with one another.

In group settings, the same process can take place, but it is complicated by human in-group tendency to maintain the *status quo*. The group will often not show much willingness to change, be resistant to considering new ideas, will often mis-perceive the ideas that are presented by communicators considered as "outsiders." The group often will express that lack of agreement in harsh terms. Whether an individual is trying to enter a group (a/B), or it is two groups engaged in communication (A/B), the tendency is to avoid change rather than be willing to consider it.

In all of this discussion of relational interactive communication within the context of education, God and His vertical relationship is an ever-present reality. For the Christian who wishes to see new ideas introduced to a group, the pathway of growth and transformation through being/belonging and becoming is a pattern that is seen in Scriptural examples like those of Paul. In Christ we live and move and have our being; He is the communication that can break the cycle of ingroup resistance.

CHAPTER 7
Relational Communication for Relational Education: Part II

TOWARD A MODEL OF RELATIONAL INTERCULTURAL EDUCATION FOR PROFESSIONAL DEVELOPMENT

Relational intercultural communication meets relational intercultural education on two levels: there is the intercultural side, which under the best of circumstances demonstrates a high interculturality. There is also the educational side, which under the best of circumstances demonstrates high quality teaching and fosters high quality learning which is both professionally sound and culturally adapted. The purpose of this chapter is to tie these two ideas into one integrated model. That one model is here being developed in terms of education but we believe that only slight modifications are necessary to also use this model for other areas of intercultural study (for instance, intercultural leadership or intercultural business).

Figure 18 provides a conceptual framework for this merging together of intercultural education with intercultural communication. This chapter will be based on the figure and will give us the opportunity to tie together many pieces that this book has introduced so far.

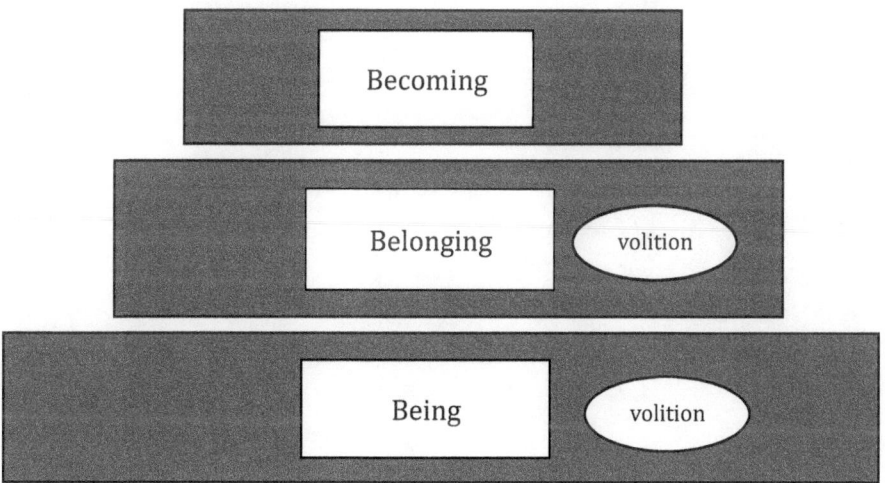

Figure 18. A Relational Model of Individual Development

Figure 18 begins with a single person who can be described by his or her characteristics of "being." That person, if they choose, can begin to interact relationally with other people in some kind of "belonging" relationship. This can be with a large, organized group or simply in a one-on-one relationship. The relationship will not normally include all of the characteristics of the person. That is why the "being" foundation is larger, longer than the graphic view of "belonging." For example, part of my "being" includes playing a musical instrument. I do not bring that "being" element into my workplace "belonging" as an educator.

Once there is a group of people involved, the individual person and the group as a whole also have an option to grow and develop or not. There are organizations (and there are people) who enjoy personal relationships without trying to grow and develop. They simply enjoy being together, and "becoming" something new is not part of the intention.

Yet there are other examples of individuals who become part of a relational group that has particular goals in mind; sports goals, or educational goals or business goals. The "becoming" part of this developmental pyramid allows us to trace the multiplication of one person as they engage with others and then choose to pursue common goals together toward a new "becoming."

Education / Growth	Description	Basic elements in educational settings
Being	The characteristics of the Beings/beings involved in the educational setting	Natural attributes, talents, interests.
Volition #1	Between being and belonging, the human will enters	If the group to which one wishes to draw near is judgmental, biased, critical it is possible that one might not have the will to engage with another group.
Belonging	Further development requires a group to work with.	Group provides motivation, resources, mentoring, accountability, correction in a healthy, appropriate relationship
Volition #2	Between belonging and becoming there is again a point of engaging the will	Growth toward "becoming" may require a positive, supportive environment to support the process of learning and growing.
Becoming	Growing attitudes, skills, knowledge, relationships	Developmental and transformational growth.

Figure 19. Relational Growth Process in Education

With this diagram in mind, let us consider the different levels in detail, first in terms of horizontal communication and then adding the reality of vertical communication.

After that we will look at the process of dynamic growth in a person first, followed by dynamic growth of an educational program. Finally, we will consider the interaction of theories of intercultural growth, comparing the RICC model with other theories that are popular in our current literature.

Level One – Being.
An individual who is growing in their intercultural relational quotient.

This is the level of Being. It reflects a person (individually at this point) who loves God and loves their neighbor as an ideal and shows a desire (volition) to grow in the ability to express, perceive and think in intercultural terms.

This person though, at the beginning of their intercultural growth, does not have experience through which to develop that ideal.

Description of Level One

We see the application of this foundational level through personal traits of openness and flexibility to new cultural patterns. On the other hand, this person is not yet experienced at cross-cultural interaction. They are at the beginning of their intercultural life. The "being" relates to skills, foundational concepts and generally open attitudes, but they may have very limited actual experience upon which to develop and grow those skills, attitudes and foundational knowledge pieces.

This is the place where we hear idealistic expressions of solidarity with other cultures. It is also the place where we hear stereotypes as people learn about cultural trends but apply those concepts wholesale without any level of interpersonal nuance. This is the person who hears about power distance, for example, and erroneously sees all people from a "high power distance" culture as fitting into a single box that low power distance cultures would call "authoritarian." Hoffman and Verdooren's statement that "cultures don't interact; people do"[101] is lost to beginners at this level simply because they lack the life-experience to see differences between people within any given culture.

Theoretical foundations of Level One –

There are a number of recent tools which provide qualitative and quantitative descriptions of a range of characteristics of a person with attributes and potential for increasing interculturality. Those tools include:

The Intercultural Relational Quotient describes a person's interculturality and intercultural potential in terms of being, closeness, cultural sensitivity, context, and influence.[102] Regularly used phrases like Emotional Intelligence, Intelligence Quotient, and the Intercultural Readiness Check are all factors within IRQ, but the IRQ concept is by design more flexible than any of those statistical measures. IRQ describes (not "measures") the personal traits of cross-cultural workers which facilitate interculturality.

The Intercultural Readiness Check[103] looks at an individual in terms of four characteristics which statistically point to successful intercultural interactions: intercultural sensitivity, intercultural communication, building commitment, and managing uncertainty.

---

[101] Diversity Competence, 2018.
[102] See Chapter 4.
[103] Brinkmann and Weerdenburg, *Intercultural Readiness*.

Long-standing tests of intelligence (IQ) are to some extent a factor for interculturality, simply because there is certainly a cognitive side to intercultural involvement.

Building on those intelligence quotients, recent literature about Cultural Intelligence (CQ)[104], and Cultural Competence also correctly see that there are levels of skill, knowledge and emotional response which are all involved in interculturality.

Level One of interculturality is always present. The person who has lived as a successful expat for years is still growing in their attitudes, knowledge and skill about culture in general and about their host culture in particular. This is the level that needs to be present in order to grow as a teacher and as a sojourner.

Level One also involves vertical relationships. God and His Word point us to attitudes of welcoming the stranger, of going to the nations, and of trusting God to be at work in and through personal relationships. Even those who do not go outside of their home culture are to have attitudes that embrace people of other cultures for the sake of the Gospel. As people develop skill, knowledge and attitudes to foster more productive horizontal relationships, they build on biblical concepts of universal sin, a Gospel that is for all people, and a coming Kingdom that includes every tribe, tongue nation and people. Models like CQ and Cultural Competence give us insight into how our horizontal relational perspectives may be tied to vertical relationships with God and with His new humanity[105].

Level Two: Belonging.
An individual who is growing in their intercultural skills, attitudes and abilities as part of a community that is different from where they grew up. This level points to applying the ideals of loving God and loving neighbor within a specific community.

Description of Level Two:

Level two moves a person from conceptual agreement to practical interaction in a specific cultural context. This is the level where the initial understanding of theoretical elements like power distance[106] or emotional variables[107] is shaped in real-world terms through the intercultural skills of

---

[104] David Livermore, *The Cultural Intelligence Difference: Master the One Skill You Can't Do Without in Today's Global Economy*, First edition. (New York: AMACOM, 2011).
[105] Stevens, *God's New Humanity: A Biblical Theology of Multiethnicity for the Church*.
[106] Hofstede, Hofstede, and Minkov, *Cultures and Organizations*.
[107] Mesquita, *Between Us*.

Self-Directed Learning[108],[109],[110], Observation[111], Asking Good Questions[112], Learning Cycle[113], etc. This is also the level where language acquisition becomes important for communication in real-life terms. It is the level where real-world vocabulary and real-world life interactions are learned through observation, trial, conversation, and error-correction.

Every schoolteacher and parent have rejoiced when their child or student realized that math does not live in books[114] but is a real skill that is used for buying groceries and adjusting cooking recipes. That same level of reality is our stage two of interculturality. The concepts that are written about in cultural sensitivity books and workshops stop being theory and are understood and applied in real life experience between a boss and their workers, or a teacher and their learners. IRQ develops through life experience, the influence of godly teachers/trainers, and God's providential involvement.

Theoretical foundations of Level Two:

This is the level where one is actively learning the realities of a specific community. It means interacting with a group of people sufficiently to first receptively and then expressively[115] interact with the ways of life of a group of people. It is where skills like observation, writing notes, confirmation of what is read in published ethnographical descriptions etc. all move outside of books and into a growing, deliberate interaction with the flesh and blood people in that community.

For a child growing up in a community of people, that learning takes place through the organic, natural growth that is referred to as enculturation. For the expat learning how to live and communicate and teach in a previously

---

[108] Jonathan Paul Lewis, *The Self-Directed Student: A Guide for Christian Vocational Development*, ed. Pamela Corvino and Alexandra Mantilla (Independently published, 2021).

[109] Malcolm S. Knowles, Elwood F. Holton III, and Richard A. Swanson, *Adult Learner: The Definitive Classic in Adult Education and Human Resource Development, The*, 8 edition. (London ; New York: Routledge, 2015).

[110] Mark Hedinger, *Culture Learning: The Art of Understanding What No One Can Teach You*, ed. Rachel Askew (CultureBound, 2021).

[111] Smith, *Creating Understanding, 2nd Edition*.

[112] Marco Blankenburgh, *The Ultimate Intercultural Question Book: 1000+ Questions to Deepen Your Intercultural Interactions* (BookBaby, 2025).

[113] Saul Mcleod, "Kolb - Learning Styles," last modified 2017, www.simplypsychology.org/learning-kolb.html.

[114] Dorothy Canfield Fisher, *Understood Betsy* (CreateSpace Independent Publishing Platform, 2014).

[115] Language acquisition and cultural adaptation in real life both begin with recognition/reception and then grow into expression.

unfamiliar culture, it is a deliberate process of learning at level one and level two. That deliberate process of learning what to others is intuitive is called acculturation.

Level Three: Becoming
The process by which a person engages in a wide range of whole life contexts within their new community in such a way that they adapt their professional skills to the host culture. The result is a growing life experience that allows professional expressions that most accurately allow perception to equate with expression.

Description of Level Three:

In our reflections about intercultural communication for intercultural education, we face two related but distinct challenges. One challenge is to enter the culture of the people so that cultural theory becomes interactive practice. This is reflected in adapting to the way of life of the host culture in areas like transportation, shopping, worship, meal preparation, interactions with government and police etc.

The other challenge is to enter professional life within the host culture. For a teacher, this might mean learning the culture sufficiently so that one can teach their area of study in a way that is both professionally accurate and culturally relevant.

This is the level of communication that needs to build on Wan's STARS[116] criteria: Scripturally Sound, Theologically Supported, Theoretically Coherent, Contextually Relevant, Practically Applicable.

This level of communication refers back to Figure 16. This figure points toward the cycle of perception-conception-volition-expression. Within one's homeland, the likelihood is that perception by an audience and expression by a communicator/teacher will be closely related. The language and cultural patterns of the two parties will closely resemble one another. Word choices, time of day, approach to delivery, amounts of homework etc. are intuitively understood in approximately the same way. The communication cycle has a limited number of "prisms" to create misunderstanding.

When the context is cross-cultural, though, that intuitive advantage is gone. Now the intuitive understanding of communicator does not naturally overlap with the intuitive understanding of listeners/audience. What is perceived is not necessarily what is expressed. What the audience thinks (conception) is not the same as what the speaker was trying to express.

---

[116] Enoch Wan, "Core Values of Mission Organizations in the Cultural Context of the 21st Century," *Global Missiology* (January 2009), www.globalmissiology.org.

Within the relationship between teacher/learner, this can show up as mismatches in areas like desired outcomes, appropriate teacher/learner relationships, word choice, preferred teaching style (rote learning compared to problem solving educational approaches), etc. The STARS approach helps to identify specific areas of difference. The communication cycle helps to show how to adjust and adapt to the communication patterns of a host culture so that educational content is expressed in a way that perception and expression are roughly equivalent.

There are two important elements to this real-world application in the world of education. We have distinguished between communication which objectifies and communication which is authentic. One of the areas that makes intercultural communication often take on that "refined", or "objectified" nature is a lack of real-life interaction. People feel artificial and overly formal when they do not have life-skill/interaction to be able to relate naturally to the people living in that host culture. Objectifying communication can happen for many reasons, but one of them is due to a simple cultural distance between an expat and the community in which they are trying to teach. It is real-life interaction outside of professional settings that allows for bridges of understanding to be built.

The importance of real-life interaction is not only true for teachers/learners. It is likewise true for the pastor or missionary for whom teaching is a normal part of life. It is true for the business professional trying to work effectively in a host culture. It is true of leaders who may understand how to lead in their home culture but do not have that understanding in their host culture. Without real life involvement and ongoing growth in cultural adaptation, it is next to impossible to move from "refined" communication (objectification) to authentic, personally engaged relational interaction/communication.

The other important element to keep in mind about real-world application of intercultural communication in an educational setting is the importance of volition. The teacher who does not wish to enter the life of their community may well speak technical truth, but they will not connect with the people they have been sent to. Bloom's[117] triad of teaching for cognitive, affective and psychomotor impact will be a cold, theoretical proposition unless there is life-interaction both within and outside of the teaching setting. Even worse, Bloom's triad will be based on the educational setting of the teacher's home culture rather than the living reality of the host culture learners. It is that fuller level of understanding that allows perception and conception to align for both teacher and learner.

---

[117] Benjamin Bloom, *Taxonomy of Educational Objectives, Book 1 Cognitive Domain* (New York: Longman, Inc., 1954).

Theoretical Foundation for Level Three:

In intercultural work, perception, conception and expression are rarely similar between the members of the dyad unless there is deliberate effort at growing in cultural and linguistic understanding. In order to approximate the same meaning between reception and expression, real life involvement is essential. To quote Donald K Smith, "communication demands involvement[118]." This is especially true when we discuss intercultural communication in terms of intercultural education.

Successful, ongoing development in levels one and two does not end even as that third level is developing. The process of growing in a new culture does not end. Acculturation is a deliberate, life-long process. Intercultural communication for intercultural education requires ongoing growth in cultural, professional, and communicative skills, knowledge and attitudes. That all takes place through healthy and deepening relationships within the host culture.

Finally, from a theoretical perspective what is true in horizontal terms is all the more true in vertical terms. To "grow in the grace and the knowledge of our Lord and Savior Jesus Christ" (2 Peter 3:18) is an intercultural process between Theo-culture and human culture that requires involvement through faith, prayer, worship, and spiritual ministry of teaching and learning. It is a cross-cultural process that is enabled by the Holy Spirit who brings perception in line with expression. God opens our minds and our hearts to His truth so that we understand Him more and more.

Beyond that, though, we recall that relational intercultural communication involves all four elements of perception, volition, conception and expression. This is true between God and people too. The importance of volition cannot be overstated. We grow in Christ when it is our desire and our will to grow in Him. God readily enters the communication cycle with us both individually and collectively. The will to learn and grow in Him is part of what we as human beings bring into that relational interaction.

Conclusion

Chapter 7 expands our model of RICC within educational contexts by incorporating a wider range of intercultural concepts. That expanded model is also made practical for individual intercultural development beyond education.

The expansion of RICC within educational settings includes three levels of intercultural growth: Level one is theoretical and attitudinal (being). Level two moves into application within a specific community where the

---

[118] Smith, *Creating Understanding*, 2nd Edition, 17.

intercultural theory becomes reality through the exercise of skill in observation, conversation, and analysis (belonging). The third level is the ongoing process of adjusting perception, conception, volition and expression to the cultural and professional realities of a teaching/learning environment. (becoming). That kind of adjustment builds upon the cultural involvement that is in focus for levels one and two.

Growing in intercultural communication for intercultural education does not end. It is a lifetime project involving all three levels of theory, community involvement, and professional development. The introduction of the qualitative concept of IRQ points to the elements of interculturality by which that lifetime of being-belonging-becoming continues to grow and develop. Chapter 8 will examine these concepts of RICC for RICE through a cross-cultural case study spanning educational settings in India and the US.

CHAPTER 8
CASE STUDY: TOWARD THE DEVELOPMENT OF AN ANALYTICAL TOOL FOR RICC

Amit Bhatia and Mark Hedinger

In this chapter, we begin with a case study that describes the educational system of India and the educational system of the United States from the lens of a single professor who has experience in both of those two educational settings. After describing the two approaches to university education, we will use them to identify some key factors to include in educational communication strategies.

The chapter then continues with a case study of communication in conflict, drawn from Acts 15.

Case Study of Education in India and the United States

Amit A. Bhatia

The purpose of this essay is to compare Indian and American systems of education through the lens of my personal experiences in each, as well as through select literature, highlighting the differing approaches to teaching and learning found in each of these educational systems.

Growing up education was of high value in my house. My earliest memories of childhood were of my parents telling me that I should become technically qualified so that I could have a lucrative career. A good education, which from their perspective meant becoming an engineer or a doctor, would help me "stand on my own feet." For that reason, the subjects which were important to master included mathematics and the sciences. This meant that other subjects such as languages, history, geography, and civics, were not as highly valued. The message I received was that I did not need to devote too much energy to their study. So, although a person could pursue other disciplines such as the humanities and commerce, a good education was one which would result in some kind of technically oriented career. This pushed me to pursue enrolling in engineering college and ultimately to studying computer science in the United States. I cannot fault my parents for espousing and inculcating in me this mindset and set of priorities, because it served as a logical response to the extremely challenging economic climate in India. Gaining a highly marketable skill in the business world by mastering computer science was just the right solution to a significant, real-world challenge.

When I moved to the US, I enrolled in a liberal arts college without fully understanding all which that entailed. I struggled with the requirement of taking courses in the humanities, thinking that a person would not be able to earn a lucrative income by studying English Literature or religion, or any such subject. This perspective was, and remains, widespread in the diaspora Indian community. For example, another Indian individual I met years later who worked as a nurse once remarked about his own children attending college that "students in the US are not as focused as 'us'." By this he was referring to college students pursuing learning by dabbling in courses in the liberal arts. However, as a college student, reading short stories, biographies, and novels in my English Literature classes began to awaken in me what I call the "human" side of me, engaging me socially, culturally, spiritually, and emotionally.

As I met and learned from students who were pursuing academic disciplines different than mine, I began to appreciate the diversity in the academic world as well as the diversity of individuals' makeup as human beings. Also, I began to understand and appreciate the differences in the foci in Indian education versus American education. I realized that education in India seems to leave a gaping hole in the development of students and that a corrective course was needed. I began to think that Indian education, rather than having a singular purpose of giving students marketable skills so that they could make a lot of money, ought instead to focus on the holistic development of each student.

Another difference I experienced in the education I received in India as compared to education I was receiving in the US was the way in which professors interacted with me in the classroom. In India there was a strict hierarchy of engagement both inside and out of the classroom. In class, the professor imparted information and I took copious notes, memorized the information, and demonstrated my learning by writing out word-for-word what I had memorized. In other words, knowledge meant memorization of the data. In the U.S. learning took place in a completely different way. I listened (and took notes), read the textbooks, and engaged the professors with what I "thought" about the information I was taking in. That is, I had the opportunity to develop critical thinking and reasoning skills, and knowledge meant developing the ability for proper application of the data I was receiving through my courses. Asking questions in the classroom was not being disrespectful of the professor, but a demonstration of the continued development of the ability to think critically. This experience foregrounded what I found to be two more deficiencies in the Indian educational system: the hierarchical power dynamics and the nearly total reliance on rote memorization.

The Indian educational system is broken up into five levels: preschool education, primary level education, secondary level education, senior secondary level education, and graduate and above level education. The first three levels are mandatory for all children aged 6 to 14 years. Prior to starting primary education, pupils are educated at the pre-primary level during which time they learn basics such as alphabets, numbers and colors as well as social skills. Secondary school education (9th and 10th grades) and the higher secondary school education (11th and 12th grades) culminate with a national or state level standardized board exam.[119] At the higher secondary level students have the option of selecting one of three streams of study: Science, which includes subjects such as Mathematics, Physics, Chemistry, Biology, Geology, and English; Commerce, which includes subjects such as Accounting, Economics, Business, Mathematics and English; and Arts, which includes subjects such as History, Political Science, Sociology, Economics, and Language. After their 10+2 (secondary schooling), a student can pursue a bachelor's, master's and, if desired, a specialized degree in a variety of disciplines of their choosing.

I was educated in India up to the Higher Secondary level, followed by one year of college-level education equivalent to the freshman year in a college in the US. During this year I studied Physics and Statistics, among other subjects, with the goal of getting a Bachelor of Science degree in Physics. The entirety of my education in India was based on the rote learning system rather than critical thinking. I developed the ability to memorize and regurgitate copious amounts of information but almost entirely missed the kind of analytical and integration skills I learned during my undergraduate and graduate level education in the US. The tiny amount of analytical exercise I was exposed to came through reading narratives in the required subjects of Hindi and English literature, but in-depth engagement with this way of thinking was disregarded and diminished because engineering colleges in India focused only on scores received in Mathematics, Physics and Chemistry for entrance into their schools.

Prabu Rajasekaran, an educational specialist whose expertise lies in helping students enhance their performance on standardized tests such as the GRE and the TOEFL, highlights seven key differences between education in India as compared to education abroad. Three of these are relevant to this essay and support my lived experience in the two educational systems.[120]

---

[119] K. P. Sheeja, "Indian School: Top Advantages of Indian Educational System," n.d., accessed October 21, 2024, https://bangalore.globalindianschool.org/blog-details/indian-school-top-advantages-of-indian-education-system.

[120] Prabu Rajasekaran, "Indian Education Vs Foreign Education: Key Differences," August 23, 2024, accessed October 21, 2024, https://www.kanan.co/blog/indian-education-vs-foreign-education/.

First, in terms of teaching methods and approaches to learning, education in India emphasizes "rote learning" as opposed to "critical thinking" in the US educational structure. Rote learning means the memorization of facts from the course textbooks and writing out this information on exams, the result of which is the memorization of information rather than understanding it. Through the Indian method of education, students become adept at "recalling details quickly" but do not learn to "think deeply about what they're learning or apply knowledge to real life. They might ace their tests but struggle to solve problems that need creative thinking or practical skills outside classroom walls." Contrast this with education in the US system that fosters the development of critical thinking and problem-solving skills. This kind of education fosters "innovation and creativity:"

Rather than simply providing answers, teachers encourage questioning, independent thinking, and finding solutions creatively. Interactive methods like group projects, discussions, and hands-on activities facilitate fun, collaborative learning experiences. This approach prepares students not just with theoretical knowledge but also equips them with practical application skills valuable for real-world challenges and teamwork in diverse settings.[121]

Second, in relation to "performance and assessment," the Indian educational system emphases grades. It is expected that students will work hard to obtain high scores on their exams because opportunities for admission into educational institutions for further education as well as employment opportunities are dependent on their marks. With an emphasis solely on exam scores, obtaining high marks by spitting out information on the exams trumps critical understanding of the subject matter. I became an expert on using logarithmic tables in Mathematics, for instance, but I still do not understand why I need to understand finding the "logs" of numbers. Rajasekaran aptly contrasts this with education in the US context, stating that:

> Schools use a mix of ways to see how well students are doing. They look at exam scores, but that's not all. Teachers also check the non-classroom performance of students such as projects, research opportunities, seminars, and essays. They watch how much you join in class and even how good you are at sports. This mix helps everyone see your full set of skills, not just what you can remember for a test.[122]

In the American approach to education, learning becomes "more about real life." Students, from the earliest grade levels, are given the opportunity to apply what they learn in the classroom to what they

---

[121] Rajasekaran. "Indian Education."
[122] Rajasekaran. "Indian Education."

experience in the "real world" through "science fairs or writing assignments that solve real problems." Education then becomes not only about getting an exam question right, but also about demonstrating that the student understands the concepts "deeply" and has learned to "use them in various parts of life." "Schools want to see creativity and critical thinking as much as they want to see high grades."[123]

Third, in terms of "career opportunities," the Indian education system focuses on theory, while education in the US put a priority on practical learning and developing innovative skills. Anil K. Rajvanshi, Director of the Nimbkar Agricultural Research Institute in Maharashtra, India, accurately criticizes the limits of theoretical education, stating that the "Indian education system seems to be producing zombies since in most of the schools, students seemed to be spending majority of their time in preparing for competitive exams rather than learning or playing."[124]

Several decades ago, the focus on core subjects – in my case, developing computer skills – seemed necessary because the Indian economy did not afford students the luxury of focusing on humanities-related subjects in their college education. A person needed to become "qualified" in a lucrative profession so that they could "stand on their feet" and to live a financially sustainable life. But now, given the impact of globalization on all societies, what was effective thirty or so years ago is no longer suitable. The lack of adequate educational development of students in India has not gone unnoticed. For instance, the Global Indian International School, seeing the need to develop students to function effectively in the global workplace, has broadened the categories of education to be included in their syllabi.[125] They are now beginning to take an holistic learning approach which moves beyond the sole focus on the core subjects in the various disciplines, focusing "more on acquiring skills in technology, communication, critical-thinking and problem solving."[126] They are also now emphasizing the significance of "cultural studies and society" so that the perspectives of students are broadened. This equips students to be able to understand issues that other societies and people face so that they become effective in addressing these issues. Furthermore, the new focus on extracurricular and co-curricular activities helps "build a student's personality and work upon his innate strengths."[127]

---

[123] Rajasekaran. "Indian Education."
[124] Anil K. Rajvanshi, "Indian Education: Creating Zombies Focused on Passing Exam," *New Indian Express*, July 3, 2013.
[125] Sheeja. "Indian School."
[126] Sheeja. "Indian School."
[127] Sheeja. "Indian School."

I am encouraged by this kind of critical reflection about the Indian educational system. I hope it will result in providing the kind of education needed to make graduates of Indian higher education institutions more effective in the intercultural, globalized world.

Case study analysis

Mark Hedinger

The comparison and contrast of Indian and USA educational settings, (including a bit of comparison between Indian education in the late 20th century with Indian education in the 2020s) gives us opportunity to describe the two systems, and to develop a tool for analysis of educational approaches in light of RICC. This analysis is not meant to be a quantitative evaluation, but rather to see the component elements that mix in what we have called "Intercultural Relational Quotient."

It is important to mention three caveats before we begin this analysis:
1) the analytical tables below only have comments where there was clear mention in Bhatia's case study. A more complex series of ethnographic descriptions would allow for greater depth of analysis.
2) The lists of theoretical measures in the left-hand column of the three tables is suggestive but not at all exhaustive. There are many other cultural variables which could also be included or could replace those listed. For example, the list below does not include any mention of Honor/Shame, Guilt/Innocence, Power/Fear[128].
3) We are describing IRQ elements, not suggesting a formal evaluation tool. In this analysis our desire is to describe what the two educational systems share in common and in what ways they differ.

The important issue in this analysis is to distinguish between culture learning which is related to characteristics, habits and thought patterns related to a person's "being" (characteristics which facilitate cultural flexibility), interactive characteristics that involve "belonging" (awareness of the variety of interactive relationships that occur across a range of communities/cultures), and practice in the iterative process of "becoming" as one learns how to communicate effectively within cultural patterns that are different than commonly found in one's homeland.

---

[128] Roland Müller, *The Messenger, the Message and the Community*, 3rd edition. (Osler, Sask.: CanBooks, 2013).

Educational Level One- Educational factors related to "being."

Theoretical Measures in educational settings	Indian educational system	American educational system
Nature of Beings/beings	Self-described as "focused" by Indian students	Seen as less focused by some Indian students
Culture	High value placed on education for sake of "standing on one's own two feet."	Education in computer science includes humanities as well as technical training
Context	Challenging economic climate	Author faced the American university as an international student.
Closeness	No mention	No mention
Influence	Technical	Social, cultural, spiritual and emotional awakening.
IRC building commitment	During college years, the author realized the importance of humanities for holistic development of each student	Multiple interests were encouraged by the American system, leading some to say that the American university is "less focused."

Figure 20. Personal attributes related to Relational Communication as seen in Amit A. Bhatia's case study

Educational Level Two – Educational factors related to "belonging."

Case study interactive traits	Indian educational system	USA educational system
Hofstede – power distance	Rote memory at teacher's order Hierarchical power dynamics	Mutual engaging between professors and students as the preferred learning style. Questions permitted.
Hofstede-Individual/Collective	Focus of education is mostly for society's benefit	Focus on individual likes/dislikes
Hofstede Achievement and Success Motivation	STEM focus (science, technology, engineering, mathematics)	Mixture of STEM and humanities
Hofstede Indulgence	Restraint is valued	Indulgence is valued
Teaching methods	Rote memory	Critical thinking
Performance and assessment	Emphasis on exams	Includes projects, classroom involvement, essays besides exams
Career development opportunities	Emphasis on theory	Emphasis on real-world problems, innovative solutions.

Figure 21. Group relational interactions seen in community through Amit A. Bhatia's case study.

Educational Level Three: educational factors related to "becoming."

Communication element	Indian educational system	USA educational system
Perception	None mentioned	None mentioned
Conception (thought process)	Independent thinking is not encouraged until after graduation	The development of critical thinking is a core value in the American education system
Volition (Will)	No mention	No mention
Expression	Rote memory and word-for-word repetition of professor's words	Students encouraged to engage in dialog. Critical thinking as a way to grow.
Iterative changes over time	Increased availability of humanities as the economic situation improved. Now "building a student's personality and working upon his innate strengths."	Educational focus on continued growth in analytical and integrative skills

Figure 22. Communication cycle for educational development (an iterative process)

These three tables (Figures 20, 21, and 22) isolate some distinct cultural patterns that vary between the US and Indian educational systems. For our case study, we can easily see several issues that an educator from India would need to adjust for successful teaching in the United States, and we can also see adjustments that a USA-American would need to make for successful teaching in India. Besides that, we notice that the Indian educational system is changing and growing as the perceived importance of STEM education is replaced by a more holistic view of education. There is not only individual growth and development, but there is also a systemic cycle of growth.

Another perspective with which to see educational elements in this case study starts with Figure 18 (being-belonging-becoming pyramid).

In the "being" level, we see student competencies and personal preferences. In years gone by, those preferences were largely set aside due to the cultural, collective need for science and technology. Students who were capable of entering engineering or other technology fields were directed into those areas even if they would have preferred another field of study. The volitional side was shaped by respect for family and culture, not by personal preference.

In the "belonging" level, we see the influence of parents and teachers within India, and later we see the influence of interactions in the American schooling system. The interpersonal relationships formed by the university student led him to see new professional options and new educational methods.

In the "becoming" level, we see spiritual, academic, and personality growth as those various influences interact with the will of the student to finally lead to an educational result that is satisfying for the student.

The value of seeing through the "being-belonging-becoming" lens is that it allows us to look at all of the different elements in figures 20, 21 and 22 and to identify the elements that are most involved in different phases of education. This, in turn, informs our communication approaches. Perception, cognition, volition and expression are shaped by who we are (including interests and aptitudes in this case study), by the groups we belong to (University student groups and interaction with professors), finally shaping the transformational end point of who we are becoming.

Case Study #2. Conflict between the church in Jerusalem and the church in Antioch. (Acts 15:1 – 35).

These same three distinctions (being, belonging, becoming) can also be used for analyzing conflictive situations. From the theoretical to the practical communication elements and then on to perception-conception-volition-expression, the opportunity for conflict is elevated in cross-cultural contexts. Acts 15:1-35 relates the story of how the church in Jerusalem responded to the growth of the church in Antioch and to the self-appointed teachers who required observance of Jewish rites and dietary laws.

Being
Acts 15 gives us a brief description of the people involved in the conflict.

The Jewish believers from Judea were of the sect of the Pharisees. They were culturally Jewish, having been raised in a strict understanding of the Law of Moses including diet, circumcision, and separation from Gentiles.

The Gentiles were less likely to value separation and exclusion.

The Jewish believers had seen signs and wonders accompany their own relationship with God through Christ, including the miracles of Pentecost plus healings and other signs.

The Gentile believers had experienced those same signs and wonders and had been instructed supernaturally to seek understanding through interaction with Jewish believing community.

Cultural Factors related to Being	Jewish Background Believers	Gentile Background Believers	Relational Observations
Nature of the people	Some Pharisees (v 5) Peter, Paul Barnabas also Jewish background	Phoenicia and Samaria in Acts 15.	Normally these two groups were not close. In Christ, they were together a "people for God's name" (15:14, 17)
Cultural patterns	Circumcision and Law of Moses (v 5). Exclusion based on diet, circumcision, faith	Not circumcised and not followers of Mosaic diet	Both to keep some basic morality (15:29) but no need for circumcision nor Mosaic dietary law
Context	Reporting to the church in Jerusalem about reception in Phoenicia and Samaria	Previous Gentile believers in Acts 10 were called clean by God in a vision to Peter (Acts 11)	A time of transition from old covenant to new covenant
Closeness	God knows the heart (v 8) – closeness with God but not necessarily with Gentile believers	Received the Holy Spirit like the Jewish background believers did	Apostles and Elders in Jerusalem call the Gentile believers "brethren" (15:23)
Influence	God's plan for Gentiles to hear the gospel and believe (v 7)	Signs and Wonders seen among Gentiles as previously among Jewish believers.	Leaders taught relationship with God first (15:17) and then with growing group of believers from other cultures (15:19-20)

Figure 23. "Being" in Jewish and Gentile Believers in Acts 15:1-35

Belonging

Acts 15 describes the cultural interactive patterns that were common to each of the groups involved in the conflict.

The Jewish believers had a background of separation from Gentiles and tight association with their own members.

The Gentiles were seen as entering into that Jewish community but without the requirements of dietary or ritual separation.

God's direction was for the Gentile believers to approach the Jewish believers for instruction. This relational step showed IRQ at work, honoring the "older brother" without losing theological precision. It also showed God at work in shaping the understanding of the Jewish believers about the relationship between old and new covenants.

Interactive Traits	Jewish background believers	Gentile background believers	Observations about development of relationship
Evidence of acceptance by God	Genealogy/descendants of Abraham	Demonstration of Holy Spirit in lives of Gentile believers	God displayed His power and wisdom by giving signs of His presence to both Jew and Gentile
Worship	The Lord your God; the Lord is One	Jesus is Lord	God poured out His Spirit to both Jewish and Gentile believers (Acts 2:18)
Basis of relationship with God	Some mistakenly thought it was obedience; Old Testament though says "the just will live by faith"	faith	Relationship with God based on faith that shows itself through works (James 2)
Reasons for relational exclusion from other people	Diet, circumcision, parentage	No cultural reasons for exclusion, but local politics or economy could cause division	To the Jews, Paul became a Jew. To the Greeks, a Greek. No reason for exclusion
Reasons for inclusion	Conversion of Gentiles to Judaism was permitted (e.g. Ruth)	Paul's teaching of being grafted into the faith of Israel	Unity in the church (Eph. 4:3-5)

Figure 24. "Belonging" in Jewish and Gentile Believers

Becoming
Acts 15 summarizes the iterative process of growth as part of a communication cycle between the parties involved, including how the conflict resolved as a result of that iterative process.

The Jewish believers grew in understanding of God's grace to both Jew and Gentile when they heard of the miracles God had done among the Gentiles.

Through James' speech, Jewish believers heard Old Testament prophets quoted as predicting this growth of God's grace among the Gentiles.

Through the ministry of Jewish believing community including Peter, Paul and Barnabas, Gentile believers understood that they were entering a community that was founded on Jewish relationships with Christ but was then expanded to Gentiles.

The result of this growth was the letter from the apostles and elders in Jerusalem to the younger church in Antioch with encouragement to remain true to the Lord, to abstain from some forms of contamination, and to be free about issues of circumcision and diet. It built relationship while also developing vertical and horizontal interculturality.

Communication Element	Gentile Believers	Jewish Believers
Perception	Joy at hearing the conversion of the Gentiles (15:3)	Gentile believers were incomplete without Mosaic Law
Conception	They heard the gospel (v 7) and God bore witness and gave the HS (v 8)	Actively taught that Gentiles needed to be circumcised to be saved (v 1) and keep Mosaic Law (v 5)
Volition	Salvation is through the grace of JC for both Jew and Gentile (v 11)	Willfully said that the Gospel only possible for those keeping the Law (v 5)
Expression	James' speech (vv 13 – 21)	None mentioned
Changes over time	Heard the gospel, believed and received HS with joy, cleansing their heart by faith (v 9)	None mentioned in this passage, but NT traces both Jewish believers who turn to Christ and others who try to mix Christ and the Law (e.g. Galatians)

Figure 25. Becoming in Jewish and Gentile Believers in Acts 15:1 - 35

Conclusion

Chapter 8 has looked at the intersection between relational communication and education through the lens of two case studies: one that compared communication factors between Indian and US American educational contexts, and one that compared Gentile and Jewish background believers in the context of Acts 15.

The analysis of the case studies is based on the elements that we have identified as part of relational interactionist school of thought applied to communication. We have identified the perception-conception-volition-expression cycle as a strong element in communication. By looking at how Indians use that cycle compared to US Americans, we noticed some key distinctions in their communication within education contexts. Similarly, by looking at the communication cycle, we found differing ways that those four elements were seen by Jewish background believers in the book of Acts compared to Gentile background believers in the same Book.

The other important element in relational interactionist theory has to do with the transformational progression of being-belonging-becoming. The progression of university students in the US into their long-term careers (a process of becoming) was notably different than the process for Indian students. Likewise, the transformational pathway for Gentile believers in the book of Acts was different than the path for Jewish background believers. By identifying the pathways of being-belonging-becoming in specific case studies we can begin to discern the specific ways that relationship (belonging) leads to change as one "becomes" something new.

The contribution of this chapter to the argument of our book is to show in real life situations how communication within relational interactionism allows for meaningful analysis to illustrate the communication cycle (perceive-conceive-will- express) and transformational progression (being-belonging-becoming).

CONCLUSION

Our Lord told us two things that are especially relevant to this book: First of all, that His Kingdom would one day include people from every tribe, tongue, nation, and people (Rev. 7:9). Secondly, He told us that our communication of His truth and His Word would be an integral part of how that final goal is reached (Acts 1:8, Matthew 28:18-20).

The volume you are reading has taken to heart both of those two elements in our attempt at creating a relational interactive approach to communication, with special focus on education. In this concluding section, we want to look back on the path we have taken and see how the elements fit together.

Element #1: Relational Interactionism

We began by saying that our intent is to see communication in a new way. Where most communication texts look at the skills and competencies of the communicators, in our case we want to look at the characteristics of the relationship between the communicators. It is not that the individual characteristics do not matter – they clearly do. But they are not isolated. There is a "both/and" thought pattern. As you read the many volumes that speak of skills, attitudes and knowledge needed to be a communicator, our desire is that along with that you also recognize that the relational patterns between people are equally important.

Element #2: Theological Perspective

From that relational interactionist perspective, then we looked at a nascent theology of communication. God the Father, Son and Spirit communicate within their own "theo-culture." They also communicate vertically with created beings including people (also including angels and demons). God's communication through Incarnation, Inspiration and Illumination gives us the choice of responding with faith (which we called Trinitarian communication) or mechanically and in self-seeking ways (which we called worldly, objectifying communication). Our biblical review of communication also extended to seeing how frequently God's Word speaks of the importance of horizontal communication. How we interact with one another as people is of great spiritual importance, as we have seen.

Element #3: Communication

The third element in our model of relational interactionist communication for education is the idea of communication. How do two or more parties communicate with one another? We have subdivided the flow of communication into several variables and then looked in depth at each one of these. The variables that are part of that relational interaction (as opposed to the communication competencies of the individuals) can be seen in figure 7. We summarize these variables below.

<u>Perception</u> of what has been received. We have seen how perception is both "objective" and related to the outside world, and internal based on our context, previous experiences, current circumstances etc. When we look at intercultural communication, the differences in perception because of differences in language and cultural expectations can make the difference between mostly understanding one another or mostly NOT understanding.

<u>Conception</u> is the word we used to describe the cognitive functions of thinking, analyzing, reflecting on what we perceive. This is an internal process, within a person. But it is flavored always by the cultural expectations and assumptions that are part of any person's internal world. We have seen that cultural expectations even shape the way that we humans think, with some of us enculturating to prefer linear, sequential thought patterns and others preferring culturally-encouraged thought patterns that look at the larger environment and the overall context in order to shape meaning.

<u>Volition</u> is our third variable, but not at all in a sequential way. Within a given person, and to an extent magnified to influence groups of people together, we speak, listen, and act according to our own will. Communication is not simply a matter of expressing facts. It is also aimed at shaping the will of the hearer.

<u>Expression</u> is the last part of our communication outline. How a person chooses to respond to a situation is the issue we find in expression. That expressive communication is heard by a listening person who will once again perceive, conceive, and exercise their will in response to the message expressed.

We talked about this model of communication and looked at how it is seen in educational settings, including formal settings and informal settings (for instance communication between a pastor and members of the congregation). The communication cycle is also at play in non-formal educational settings like workshops or seminars. It is important to note that the same cycle of communication could also be seen in many other professional and real-life settings.

Element #4: Relationality

Our first element in this study was "relational interactionism." That was an appropriate foundation for our model of communication. Nestled within that overall theoretical framework is the idea of relationality. To be brief, the question behind relationality is, "what do we mean by relationship?"

We answered that question by contrasting with the world's view of relationship as an idiomatic expression meaning "friendship" or "romantic interest." We are not talking about that *per se*.

What we are talking about is the complexity of relationship as seen by the different factors that affect any given relationship on any given day. We looked at Natalie Kim's identification of core factors in describing a relationship: the nature of the beings/Beings, the context, the cultural expectations, the level of closeness, and the influence that affects one or both of the partners.

Relationality also makes us realize that there are healthy, positive relationships and there are also negative, harmful relationships. Those same five characteristics become a good outline for better understanding the nature of a relationship itself as well as how that relationship affects the people involved.

Element #5: Transformation

Issues of change and transformation are core issues for educators. Building on our model of interactive relational communication, we then asked how relationships bring about change to the people involved. We distinguished between two types of change: transformational change which encourages positive growth in godliness, and transgressional change which encourages responses which the bible refers to as sinful and fleshly.

We looked at some models of transformational change from the perspective of interactive relational thought. We especially built on the picture of being (our human characteristics at the individual level), belonging (the role of interaction in community) and becoming (the process of change of a person in spiritual and physical ways.)

Figure 17 and 18 in the text highlights some of the details in this progression from individual being to community belonging and on to transformational becoming.

Element #6: IRQ - a tool for describing relational interactionist communication

Finally, our text includes two tools meant to provide a framework for evaluating communication within a given set of relationships.

First we looked at the IRQ – the Intercultural Relational Quotient, as suggested by Hannah Keppler. Her perspective is that there are numerous forces at work within the relationships found in human communication. We do well to create a model of analysis and evaluation that permits us to identify which ones may be most active in any given communication environment. Whereas other communication approaches look at personal competencies (which do have a place), the IRQ approach allows each situation to be defined in its own right. Communication between a teacher and student in a special-needs classroom will be different than communication in an educational setting of graduate classes for adults. The IRQ allows us to define those two situations on their own merits.

The second tool that we used to analyze communication within a given context was presented through the two case studies of Chapter 8. In one case, we looked at the comparison and contrast of educational settings in India in the 1990s, India in the 2020s, and the United States. The analysis of that case study highlighted how communication, relationship, and transformation are all at play in different ways. The analysis also highlighted some practical ways that educators from India might need to adjust for opportunities in the US, and vs versa.

Along with that case study from the world of intercultural education we also looked at a case study of cross-cultural conflict from Acts 15. Once again, by looking at communication through the lens of relationship we were able to see some specific IRQ elements that were involved in the conflict and its resolution. The gap between perception, conception, volition and expression between the Gentile believers and the Jewish-background believers became a way for us to illustrate and gain skill in the use of our relational interactive model for communication in the context of education.

This volume is presented to introduce a concept, not to give the final word. In days to come we welcome involvement by students and practitioners of intercultural communication and of intercultural education.

In the meantime, our own perception is that communication is both vertical and horizontal and we ask God to take these concepts and multiply them for His kingdom's sake. Our conception is that interactive communication helps us to better understand the transformative power of communication as we consider being-belonging-becoming. The expressions we have shared are our attempts at capturing the flow of these multiple ideas of relationality, interculturality, communication, and education. And our will is that we be honoring to the God in whom we live and move and have our being.

APPENDIX

Publications by the Center of Diaspora & Relational Research (CDRR) Western Seminary Press or Western Academic Publishers

Relational Book Series

Chiu, Noel, and Enoch Wan. *Establishing Frontline LGBTQ Outreach: An Exploratory Study*. Western Academic Publishers, 2022.

Early, Alex, and Enoch Wan. *The Cross and the Kaleidoscope: Substitutionary Atonement and Our Relationships*. Western Academic Publishers, 2021.

Gimple, Ryan, and Enoch Wan. *Covenant Transformative Learning: Theory and Practice for Mission*. Western Academic Publishers, 2021.

Wan, Enoch, and Christopher M. Santiago. *Motivations for Mission: A Relational-Covenantal Perspective*. Western Academic Publishers, 2022.

Wan, Enoch, and Jace Cloud. *Doxological Missiology: Theory, Motivation, and Practice*. Western Academic Publishers, 2022.

Wan, Enoch, and John Jay Flinn. *Holistic Mission through Mission Partnership: An Instrumental Case Study in La Ceiba, Honduras*. Western Academic Publishers, 2021.

Wan, Enoch, and John Ferch. *Relational Leadership Development: An Ethnological Study in Inuit Contexts*. Western Academic Publishers, 2022.

Wan, Enoch, and Jon Raibley. *Transformational Change in Christian Ministry*. Second Edition. Portland, Oregon: Western Academic Publishers, 2022.

Wan, Enoch, Mark Hedinger, and Jon Raibley. *Relational Intercultural Education for Intercultural Ministry*. Western Academic Publishers, 2024.

Wan, Enoch, Mark Hedinger, and Jon Raibley. *Transformational Growth: Intercultural Leadership/Discipleship/Mentorship*. Western Academic Publishers, 2023.

Wan, Enoch, and Mathew Karimpanamannil. *A Theology of Spirit-Anointed Witness in Holistic Christian Mission Framed in the Relational Paradigm*. Western Press, 2019.

Wan, Enoch, and Shane Mikeska. *Engaging the Secular World through Life-on-Life Disciple-Making in the British Context: Relational Paradigm in Action*. Western Seminary Press, 2020.

Wan, Enoch, and Tin Nguyen. *A Holistic and Contextualized Mission Training Program: Equipping Lay Leaders for Local Mission in Vietnam*. Western Academic Publishers, 2022.

Wan, Enoch, and Joshua Paxton. *Relational Partnerships for Missions Mobilization*. Portland: Western Academic Publishers, 2022.

Wan, Enoch, and Rob Penner. *Missionary Preparation in The Gospel Of Matthew in Light of 28:16-20: A Narrative and Relational Study*. Western Academic Publishers, 2022.

BIBLIOGRAPHY

Arasaratnam, Lily A., and Marya L. Doerfel. "Intercultural Communication Competence: Identifying Key Components from Multicultural Perspectives." *International Journal of Intercultural Relations* 29, no. 2 (March 2005): 137–163.

Bateson, Gregory. *Steps to an Ecology of Mind*. Ballantine book. New York: Ballantine Books, 1972.

Bennett, Milton. "Developmental Model of Intercultural Sensitivity (DMIS)." *International Journal of Intercultural Relations* 10, no. 2 (n.d.).

Blankenburgh, Marco. *The Ultimate Intercultural Question Book: 1000+ Questions to Deepen Your Intercultural Interactions*. BookBaby, 2025.

Bloom, Benjamin. *Taxonomy of Educational Objectives, Book 1 Cognitive Domain*. New York: Longman, Inc., 1954.

Brinkmann, Ursula, and Oscar van Weerdenburg. *Intercultural Readiness: Four Competences for Working across Cultures*, 2014.

Brooks, Arthur C. *From Strength to Strength: Finding Success, Happiness, and Deep Purpose in the Second Half of Life*. New York: Portfolio, 2022.

Brown, Colin. *The New International Dictionary of New Testament Theology*. Vol. 3. Grand Rapids, Mich.: Zondervan, 1975.

Chan, Sonia. "A Relational Model of Intercultural Learning and Interactions." In *Transformational Change in Christian Ministry*, edited by Enoch Wan and Jon Raibley, 157–61. Western Academic Publishers, 2022.

Dehaene, Stanislas. *How We Learn: Why Brains Learn Better Than Any Machine . . . for Now*. Penguin Books, 2020.

Donati, Pierpaolo. *Relational Sociology: A New Paradigm for the Social Sciences*. Routledge, 2012.

Dunbar, R.I.M. "Coevolution of Neocortical Size, Group-Size and Language in Humans." *Behavioral and Brain Sciences* 16 (1992): 681–694.

Elwell, Walter A., ed. *Evangelical Dictionary of Theology*. Baker reference library. Grand Rapids, Mich.: Baker Book House, 1984. Accessed January 31, 2025. https://covers.openlibrary.org/b/id/6623103-M.jpg.

Fisher, Dorothy Canfield. *Understood Betsy*. CreateSpace Independent Publishing Platform, 2014.

Griffin, Em, Andrew M. Ledbetter, and Glenn G. Sparks. *A First Look at Communication Theory 10th Edition*. 10th edition. McGraw-Hill Education, 2018.

Gunton, Colin E. *The Promise of Trinitarian Theology*. London: T&T Clark, 2003.

Hall, Edward T. *The Silent Language*. [1st ed.]. Garden City, New York: Doubleday & Company, Inc., 1959. Accessed January 31, 2025. https://archive.org/details/silentlanguage00hall.

Hedinger, Mark. *Culture Learning: The Art of Understanding What No One Can Teach You*. Edited by Rachel Askew. CultureBound, 2021.

Hiebert, Paul G. *Cultural Anthropology*. Philadelphia: Lippincott, 1976.

Hoffman, Dr Edwin, and Arjan Verdooren. *Diversity Competence: Cultures Don't Meet, People Do*. Illustrated edition. Wallingford ; Boston: CABI, 2019.

Hofstede, Geert, Gert Jan Hofstede, and Michael Minkov. *Cultures and Organizations: Software of the Mind, Third Edition*. 3 edition. New York: McGraw-Hill Education, 2010.

Imahori, T. Todd, Mary L. Lanigan, Lily A. Arasaratnam, and Marya L Doerfel. "Intercultural Communication Competence: Identifying Key Components from Multicultural Perspectives." *International Journal of Intercultural Relations* 29, no. 2 (March 2005): 137.

Imahori, T.Todd, and Mary L. Lanigan. "Relational Model of Intercultural Communication Competence." *Special Issue: Intercultural Communication Competence* 13, no. 3 (January 1, 1989): 269–286.

James, ed., Ross W. *Case Studies in Christian Communication in an Asian Context*. Mandaluyong, Philippines: OMF Literature, Inc., 1989.

Katan, David, and Mustapha Taibi. *Translating Cultures: An Introduction for Translators, Interpreters and Mediators*. 3rd edition. Routledge, 2021.

Kinlaw, Dennis F. *Let's Start with Jesus: A New Way of Doing Theology*. Grand Rapids, Mich: Zondervan Academic, 2005.

Knowles, Malcolm S., Elwood F. Holton III, and Richard A. Swanson. *Adult Learner: The Definitive Classic in Adult Education and Human Resource Development, The*. 8 edition. London ; New York: Routledge, 2015.

Leung, Kwok, Soon Ang, and Mei Ling Tan. "Intercultural Competence." *Annual Review of Organizational Psychology and Organizational Behavior* (2014): 490.

Lewis, Jonathan Paul. *The Self-Directed Student: A Guide for Christian Vocational Development*. Edited by Pamela Corvino and Alexandra Mantilla. Independently published, 2021.

Livermore, David. *The Cultural Intelligence Difference: Master the One Skill You Can't Do Without in Today's Global Economy*. First edition. New York: AMACOM, 2011.

Luna, David, Torsten Ringberg, and Laura A. Peracchio. "One Individual, Two Identities: Frame Switching among Biculturals." *Journal of Consumer Research* 35, no. 2 (August 1, 2008): 279–293. Accessed October 3, 2024. https://doi.org/10.1086/586914.

Mcleod, Saul. "Kolb - Learning Styles." Last modified 2017. www.simplypsychology.org/learning-kolb.html.

Mesquita, Batja. *Between Us: How Cultures Create Emotions*. New York, NY: W. W. Norton & Company, 2022.

Meyer, Erin. *The Culture Map*. New York: PublicAffairs, 2016.

Moreau, A. Scott, Evvy Hay Campbell, and Susan Greener. *Effective Intercultural Communication (Encountering Mission): A Christian Perspective*. 1st edition. Grand Rapids, MI: Baker Academic, 2014.

Müller, Roland. *The Messenger, the Message and the Community*. 3rd edition. Osler, Sask.: CanBooks, 2013.

Rajasekaran, Prabu. "Indian Education Vs Foreign Education: Key Differences," August 23, 2024. Accessed October 21, 2024. https://www.kanan.co/blog/indian-education-vs-foreign-education/.

Rajvanshi, Anil K. "Indian Education: Creating Zombies Focused on Passing Exam." *New Indian Express*, July 3, 2013.

Rathje, Stefanie. "Intercultural Competence: The Status and Future of a Controversial Concept." *Language and Intercultural Communication* 7, no. 4 (April 4, 2007). Accessed March 25, 2024. https://papers.ssrn.com/abstract=1533596.

Rogers, Everett M, and Thomas M Steinfatt. *Intercultural Communication*. Long Grove, IL: Waveland Press, Inc., 1999.

Rogers, L. Edna, and Valentín Escudero, eds. *Relational Communication: An Interactional Perspective To the Study of Process and Form*. 1st edition. Mahwah, NJ: Routledge, 2003.

Ross, Lee, David Greene, and Pamela House. "The 'False Consensus Effect': An Egocentric Bias in Social Perception and Attribution Processes." *Journal of Experimental Social Psychology* 13, no. 3 (May 1977): 279–301. Accessed October 4, 2024. https://linkinghub.elsevier.com/retrieve/pii/002210317790049X.

Schaeffer, Francis. *The Complete Works of Francis A Schaeffer: Volume 1: A Christian View of Philosophy and Culture*. Westchester IL: Crossway Books, 1982.

Schriefer, Paula. "What's the Difference between Multicultural, Intercultural, and Cross-Cultural Communication?," April 18, 2016. https://springinstitute.org/whats-difference-multicultural-intercultural-cross-cultural-communication/.

Sheeja, K. P. "Indian School: Top Advantages of Indian Educational System," n.d. Accessed October 21, 2024. https://bangalore.globalindianschool.org/blog-details/indian-school-top-advantages-of-indian-education-system.

Smith, Donald K. *Creating Understanding, 2nd Edition*. 2nd ed. edition. Artists in Christian Testimony International LLC, 2022.

Stevens, David E. *God's New Humanity: A Biblical Theology of Multiethnicity for the Church*. Eugene, OR: Wipf and Stock Publishers, 2012.

Tira, Sadiri Joy. *From Womb to Tomb: Generational Missiology in the 21st Century and Beyond*. PageMaster Publishing, 2024.

Trompenaars, Alfons, and Charles Hampden-Turner. *Riding the Waves of Culture: Understanding Diversity in Global Business*. London; Boston: Nicholas Brealey Publishing, 2015.

Wan, Enoch. "Core Values of Mission Organizations in the Cultural Context of the 21st Century." *Global Missiology* (January 2009). www.globalmissiology.org.

———. "Interculturality and Intercultural Education: The Concept and Definition of 'Culture' at Two Levels." Western Seminary, 2022.

———. "Rethinking Urban Mission in Terms of Spiritual and Social Transformational Change." Virtual: Missiological Society of Ghana/WAMS Biennial International Conference, October 26, 2021.

———. "The Paradigm of 'Relational Realism.'" *Occasional Bulletin* 19, no. 2 (2006): 4.

Wan, Enoch, and Jace Cloud. *Doxological Missiology: Theory, Motivation, and Practice*. Western Academic Publishers, 2022.

Wan, Enoch, and Mark Hedinger. *Relational Missionary Training: Theology, Theory & Practice*. Edited by Kendi Howells Douglas, Stephen Burris, and Jen Johnson. Urban Loft Publishers, 2020.

Wan, Enoch, Mark Hedinger, and Jon Raibley. *Relational Intercultural Education for Intercultural Ministry*. Portland, OR: Western Academic Publishers, 2024.

———. *Transformational Growth: Intercultural Leadership/Discipleship/Mentorship*. Western Academic Publishers, 2023.

Wan, Enoch, and Natalie Kim. *Relational Intercultural Training for Practitioners of Business As Mission: Theory and Practice*. Western Academic Publishers, 2022.

Wan, Enoch, and Jon Raibley. *Transformational Change in Christian Ministry*. 2nd edition. Portland, OR: Western Academic Publishers, 2022.

Wan, Enoch Yee-nock. *Diaspora Missiology: Theory, Methodology, and Practice*. 2nd ed. Portland, Or.: Institute of Diaspora Studies : Western Seminary, 2014.

Zotzmann, Karin. "The Impossibility of Defining and Measuring Intercultural Competencies." In *Resistance to the Known: Counter-Conduct in Language Education*, edited by Damian J. Rivers, 168–191. London: Palgrave Macmillan UK, 2015. https://doi.org/10.1057/9781137345196_8.

www.ingramcontent.com/pod-product-compliance
Lightning Source LLC
Chambersburg PA
CBHW050906160426
43194CB00011B/2315